ACTION GUIDE SERIES

TINNA C. NIELSEN • LI

Action Guide
Inclusion Nudges for Leaders

in all organisations and communities

INCLUSION NUDGES

30 Inclusive Actions
Enhancing your leadership by leveraging all diverse human potential
and de-biasing systems, cultures, and behaviours

Stand out as a leader by applying Inclusion Nudges
and making inclusion the norm – everywhere, for everyone

Authors of The Inclusion Nudges Guidebook (2020)
Authors of the Inclusion Nudges Action Guide Series
Founders of the Inclusion Nudges Global Initiative & Community
www.inclusion-nudges.org
contact@inclusion-nudges.org

Tinna C. Nielsen
Founder, Move the Elephant for Inclusiveness
www.movetheelephant.org

Lisa Kepinski
Founder, Inclusion Institute
www.inclusion-institute.com

Inclusion Nudges for Leaders Action Guide
August 2020
© Tinna C. Nielsen & Lisa Kepinski
ISBN: 9798679411777
KDP

Book cover art & icon design by Ruth Crone Foster
www.ruthcronefoster.dk
Book design by Christina Hucke
www.christinahucke.de

INCLUSION NUDGES

Good leadership
is leading inclusively.

This Action Guide
makes it easy for you to do.

Table of Contents

What Leaders Say About Inclusion Nudges	7
Section 1: **Good Leadership Is Leading Inclusively**	13
Section 2: **The Power of Inclusion Nudges**	41
Section 3: **Inclusive Actions for Leaders**	49
Section 4: **How You Take This Forward**	221
Reference Section	237
About the Authors	239
Endnotes	242

....

The majority of the actions in this Action Guide are from The Inclusion Nudges Guidebook *(2020) by Lisa Kepinski & Tinna C. Nielsen.*

To learn more about the Inclusion Nudges global initiative and community, go to the website. There you will find more resources to support you, including about The Inclusion Nudges Guidebook *and the other books in the Action Guide Series.*

Learn more at the Inclusion Nudges resource platform
www.inclusion-nudges.org

The Inclusion Nudges Global Initiative & Change Approach

Let's make inclusion the norm – everywhere, for everyone

Why
There is a need to leverage the diverse human potential of everyone to co-create inclusive organisations, communities, and society

What
Inclusion Nudges are behavioural designs to debias and enhance inclusive collaboration, leadership, development, and decisions

How
Empowering you to apply Inclusion Nudges to engage all people in making systems, cultures, and behaviours inclusive as the norm

INCLUSION NUDGES

What LEADERS say about INCLUSION NUDGES

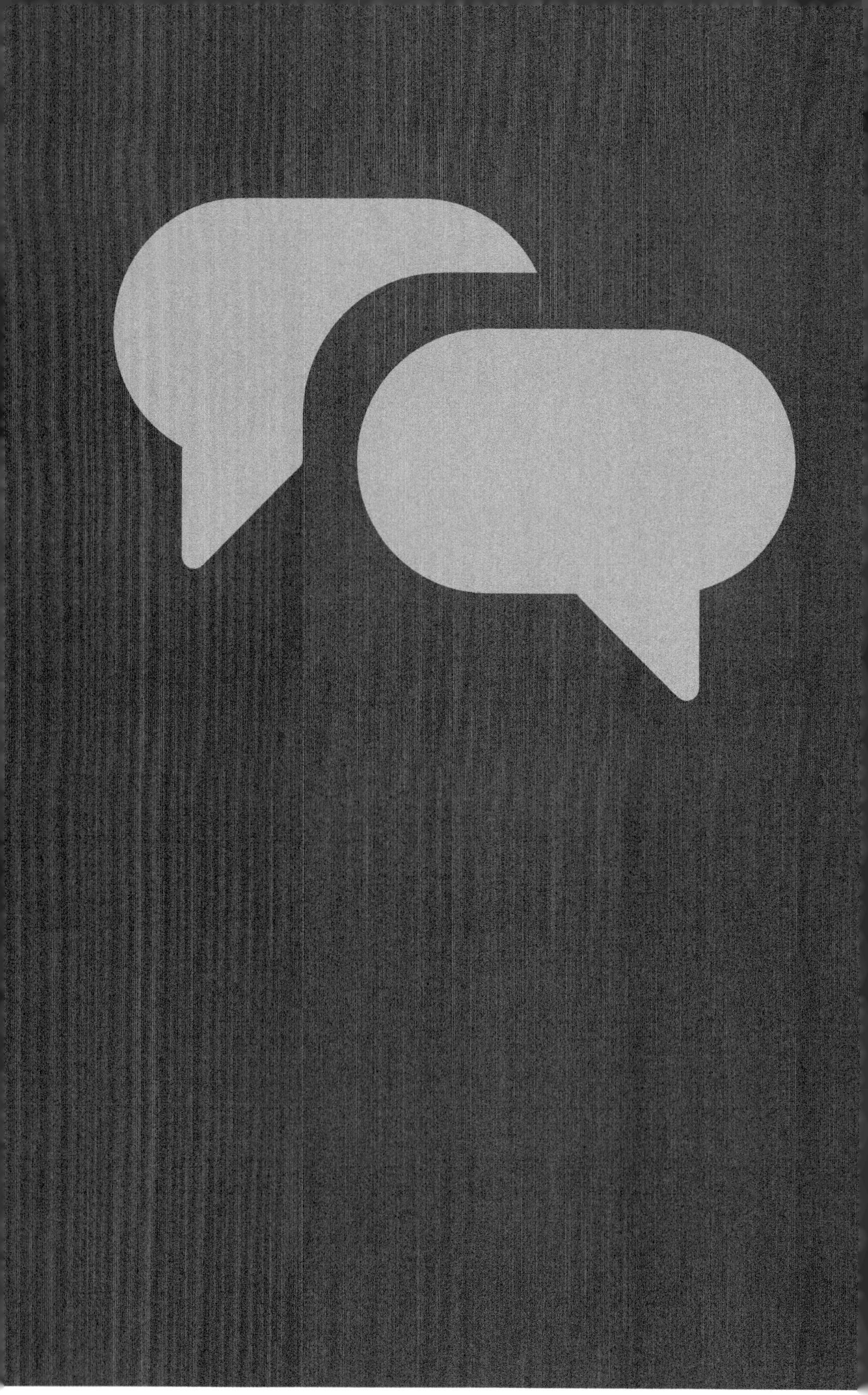

"*The Inclusion Nudges Guidebook* shows how practitioners can use behavioral insights to create more inclusive, more diverse, and better organizations. I recommend it to all who care and want to make a difference."

Iris Bohnet
Albert Pratt Professor of Business & Government and
Co-director, Women & Public Policy Program
Kennedy School of Government, Harvard University, U.S.

"Many people now understand bias but are still searching for truly effective ways to reduce it. This refreshing and timely book is filled with behavioral science-based practical examples, referred to as 'Inclusion Nudges', that are designed for easy use by people in their organizations and communities to de-bias, reduce harassment and create greater inclusion. It's time to move from discussing to acting, and that's what *The Inclusion Nudges Guidebook* will help you to do."

Amy Cuddy
Social psychologist, author, speaker, & Harvard University lecturer, U.S.

"After so much communication by experts and 'sponsors' to state the importance of diversity and after so many hours of D&I training to increase the awareness, I always wondered how long-lasting change in behaviour can be truly achieved. Tinna and Lisa's full version of *The Inclusion Nudges Guidebook* not only gives some idea, but it provides a very well structured and supported reference library of 100 potential solutions. And do you still feel stuck to make the change? Detailed stuck patterns are included!"

Endre Szabo
Senior Vice President, Managing Director, Developing Europe & Africa Region
Brown-Forman, The Netherlands

"Tinna Nielsen and Lisa Kepinski have grabbed the tiger the tail with their excellent work on Inclusion Nudges. By doing exhaustive research on not only what can work, but also what is actually working, they have put together a powerful toolkit that not only helps people discover behaviors that can encourage a more inclusive environment, but also shapes our thinking in ways that help us learn to find new solutions ourselves. This is an important book for anyone who wants to create real, sustainable change in their organization."

Howard Ross
Founder Cook Ross, author, consultant, & speaker, Founder Udarta Consulting, U.S.

"Inclusion is one of the most important things to be mindful of in the tech industry. Stereotypes may influence with whom and how we may work. It is a waste of potential, resources, and money, not to include everyone. It is our responsibility as leaders, founders, and C-levels to include everyone in our organisations. It's not only about team building; it is also about growing the company. There is no growth without the team. There is no team without inclusion. The Inclusion Nudges approach offers many ways to make this happen in our organisations. I have used some of these approaches to great impact within my own company, and I encourage others to try this as well."
Bartek Jazwinski
Co-founder, Perfect Dashboard, Poland

"What if we're going about this inclusion thing all wrong? This the gently persuasive idea behind Inclusion Nudges...co-founded by Lisa Kepinski and Tinna Nielsen, two experts who were looking for a better way. They share what they learn freely and invite others to do the same via their open-source platform ... I plan to nudge my way to a more open mind. We all should."[1]
Ellen McGirt
Senior Editor, Fortune Magazine & Co-chair, The CEO Initiative, U.S.

"As a D&I professional that is often asked to conduct presentations, lead meetings or just break the ice, this book will be invaluable to me. I highly recommend it for people leaders. It is laid out in such a way that anyone can pick it up and easily find a "nudge" that will help to start the conversation around inclusion and diversity. A must have in any leadership toolbox."
Kevin Bradley
Senior Advisor, Global Inclusion & Diversity, Zebra Technologies, U.S.

"*The Inclusion Nudges Guidebook* is my go-to resource to create behavioral nudges to increase diversity, mitigate bias, and create a culture of belonging. The nudges are practical, easy to apply or adapt, and based on the science of how our brains work. Whether diversity and inclusion is your full-time job or you are a business leader that cares deeply about this topic, this book gives you the most bang for your buck!"
Scott Ballina
Senior Director, Diversity & Inclusion, Citrix, U.S.

"Governments around the world are more and more considering and using behavioural insights to improve the lives of citizens. *The Inclusion Nudges Guidebook* is a good resource for public servants interested in learning more about how to have a more inclusive society."

Lisa Witter
Executive Chairperson and Co-founder, Apolitical, Germany

"Inclusion Nudges are the innovation we need today & a blueprint for a future in which we are desiging organisations and communities to be more inclusive from the get-go rather than as an overlay or afterthought."

Minjon Tholen
Chief Inclusion & Strategic Innovation Officer, Amnesty International, U.S.

"Leaders can embody social courage through their workplace actions. A first step is to implement Inclusion Nudges. Sounds too simple perhaps but the results are profound."

Jo Ann Morris
Founder of Integral Coaching,
Author of *Ignite: Inspiring Courageous Leaders*, and
Co-Founder of White Men as Full Diversity Partners, U.S.

"Inclusion Nudges help enable leaders to move from general awareness to catalyst agents for inclusion & diversity ... the ideas are simple and immediately actionable, with several members of my team immediately incorporating changes in their day to day leadership."

Kaye DeLange
Vice President for Salt Business Operations and Supply Chain Leader, Cargill, U.S.

"Many leaders believe that creating a more inclusive workplace requires costly D&I programs and massive culture change efforts over months or years. This action guide with Inclusion Nudges for leaders contains 30 powerful and proven actions that have an extraordinary impact and can be done today for very little investment. Like the Inclusion Nudges themselves, this small yet powerful book has a disproportionately high ROI and is a vital part of the modern leaders' toolkit."

Guy Martin
Global HR Program Director, ASSA ABLOY Global Solutions

SECTION 1

Good Leadership Is Leading Inclusively

> Getting this right, pays off.
> But only when you change some absurd realities.

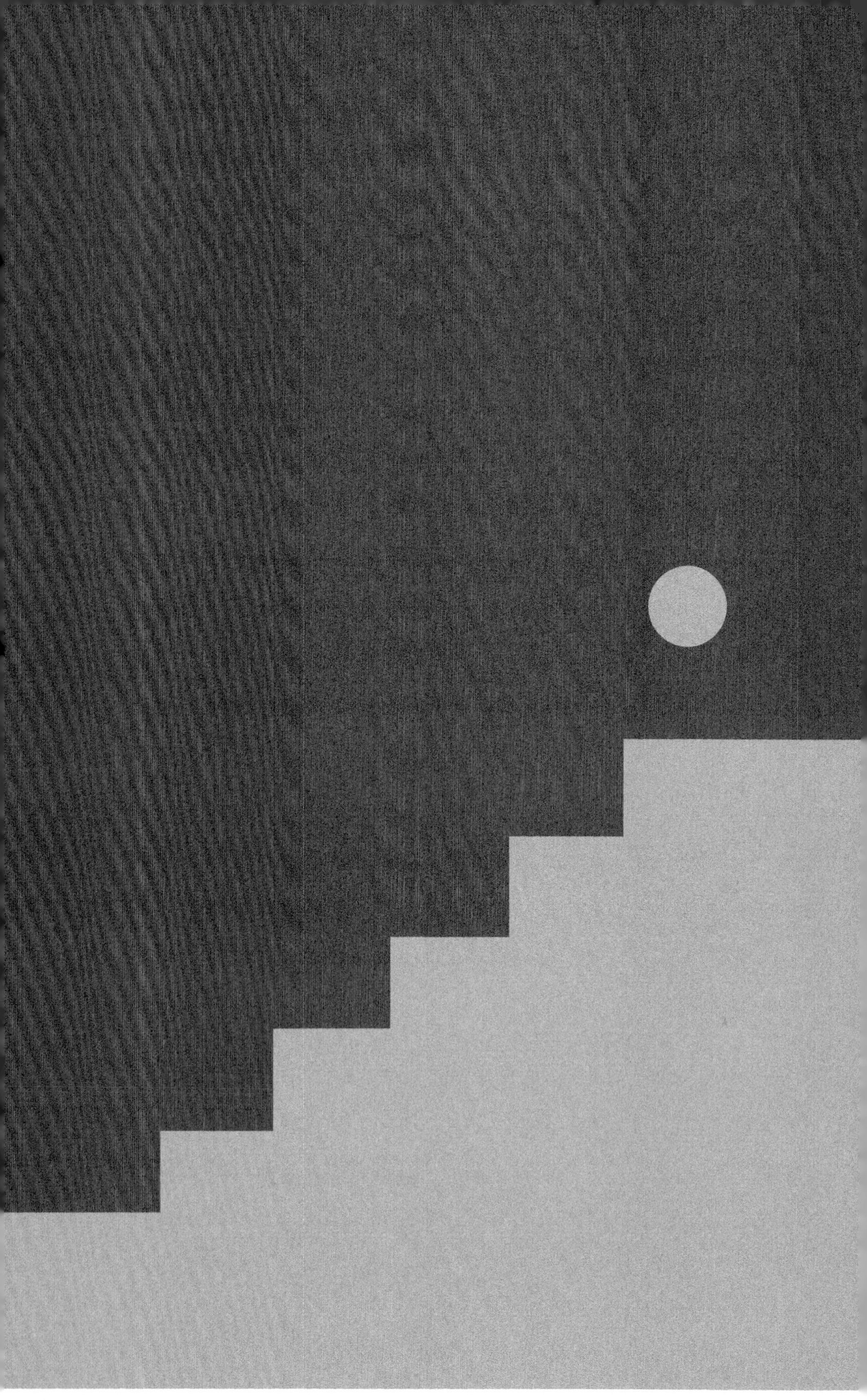

A scenario based on reality

Have you ever met a leader or project manager saying,

"I always make sure to waste the talent of the people in my team by facilitating meetings and idea-generation in ways that make them all think the same and shut up. Diversity is a waste of time and critical thinking is a pain!"

We haven't! But in our work as leaders and change makers for inclusion, we, the authors Tinna C. Nielsen and Lisa Kepinski, have seen behaviours that result in this reality playing out again and again. Unfortunately, it's the norm that most meetings, group idea-generation sessions, decision-making, new product or services creation, and strategy development are facilitated in ways that lead to the waste of diverse human talent and collective potential of the group. And this happens without intention. As a matter of fact, the intention is mostly the opposite.

Many leaders repeatedly state that it is important that everyone speaks their mind, shares their views, and expresses their critical thoughts. Having a variety of people in a group and ensuring they can contribute reduces the impact of groupthink[2] and improves decision-making.[3] We all know exactly how important this is for the group's ability to develop new solutions, solve tasks, and address problems.[4] By now, most leaders have heard about the research on the benefits of inclusive participation and cultures, as well as how it improves engagement, health, performance, and innovation.[5] We know how important it is for organisations and communities that people feel empowered and have opportunities to contribute with their talents and views. Workplaces are measuring it regularly through employee engagement surveys and other metrics. Yet while the intentions are good, a 'just speak up' approach has hidden barriers to getting access to a diverse input of perspectives. It is simply not enough to tell people to 'speak up'.

Hidden barriers

This is due to invisible and unintentional group dynamics, formal and informal power, status and roles in a group, self-silencing, and much more. Evidence from a wide body of research has proven over and over that group dynamics, such as group conformity, influence heavily in situations of collaboration and decision-making. Research and experiments on conformity[6] show that group dynamics are a powerful force that makes individuals conform to the opinion of the majority. The findings show that more than a third of people on average will conform to the views of the majority, even when knowing the view or proposed solution is wrong. As social beings we have an innate, basic need to be and feel accepted by the group. We conform unconsciously – and sometimes consciously. We conform due to a fear of social sanctioning and punishment, as well as out of concern for our reputation. We conform because we are afraid of being perceived as incompetent or because we believe that what the majority of our peers think must be right. This means that we don't disclose nor share information or opinions that depart from the group's inclination.

> We tend to believe that if we encourage people to share their views and beliefs candidly, then they will do so. Similarly, most of us genuinely believe we are independent individuals who will speak up even if the majority of others in the group have a different view than us. But we tend not to.

Speaking up in a group can be a vulnerable situation for many people. Especially when having a point of view that differs from the majority. We hold back from speaking even when we know in our rational mind that speaking first does not make someone else more right than the others in a group. We stay quiet even when we know that if the majority quickly agrees on something it does not make them more right. Nevertheless, we behave as if it does when we conform to the majority view and through our own self-silencing.

Facilitating group work in ways where people are encouraged to speak up and engage in constructive discussion, can easily become a case of the loudest gets heard. It often favours people with communication styles that match the cultural norms (such as extrovert), those with the most power and status, and members of the majority. These factors can result in less input and make it easier to remain silent and go along with a view already expressed.

> All these mental and social mechanisms limit access to the diversity of perspectives and human potential that is so crucial in task solving, innovation, and decision making.

The invisible gap

Surely, no leaders who perceive themselves to be professional leaders, who have put together a team or group of great people to solve shared tasks and challenges, who have developed a new strategy, service, or product, or who want to make good decisions, would have a deliberate intention to waste the skills, know-how, passion, knowledge, and ideas of all these people. Nor would any leader with their conscious and rational mind believe that making people shut up, stop thinking as individuals, and diminish their ability to use critical thinking, are the best ways to achieve creativity, innovation, engagement, and great, new solutions. This defies rational belief, doesn't it?

There is a gap between our intentions and actions because there is a gap between two interdependent modes of thinking in our mind, and because there are a lot of blind spots. So, the absurd scenario we outlined in the very beginning of this book is not fictional.

> What seems to be an absurd scenario of wasting diverse human potential, is in fact an absurd reality that we create and live everyday because of how our unconscious mind works.
>
> When left unaddressed, it gets replicated time and time again in our organisations and communities, without any conscious intentions.

How to close the gap

There is hope. It's actually easy to close this gap by applying these behavioural insights. Scientific conformity experiments show that people go along with the group norms less when they are asked to write their perspectives before hearing the views of the others in the group or to share them with a peer before talking in plenary. Researchers conclude that this is due to having less at stake and ensuring psychological safety.

Psychological safety is a mental condition in which human beings feel included, safe to learn, safe to contribute, and safe to challenge the status quo without fear of being embarrassed, marginalised, or sanctioned in any way.[7] Psychological safety is also a shared belief that the team is safe for interpersonal risk taking.[8] It all comes down to being able to show and employ one's self without fear of negative consequences of self-image, status, or career.[9] This is a critical foundation for creating an inclusive and innovative culture.

Leveraging diverse human potential?
This brings us to the purpose of leveraging the human potential of everyone and the diversity in our organisations and communities.

How can we possibly succeed with that if we have such a profound and hidden gap between our rational understanding and our behaviour?

What implications does this have for our leadership? And what is the impact on people, our organisations, and communities?

> How can we all contribute to making inclusive cultures and behaviours the norm in everything we do?
>
> It starts with understanding the human mind better and knowing exactly how to change the shortcoming into strength with very specific actions, such as the 30 examples in this book.

Let's take a closer look at our thinking systems and how the human mind can be a barrier to realising our intentions for leading and facilitating inclusively and making sound decisions.

Important insights about the human mind

The human mind is not one unified system of thinking. It has two interdependent modes of thinking. One is the unconscious, automatic system (1) and the other is the conscious, reflective system (2). See the distinction in the following illustration.

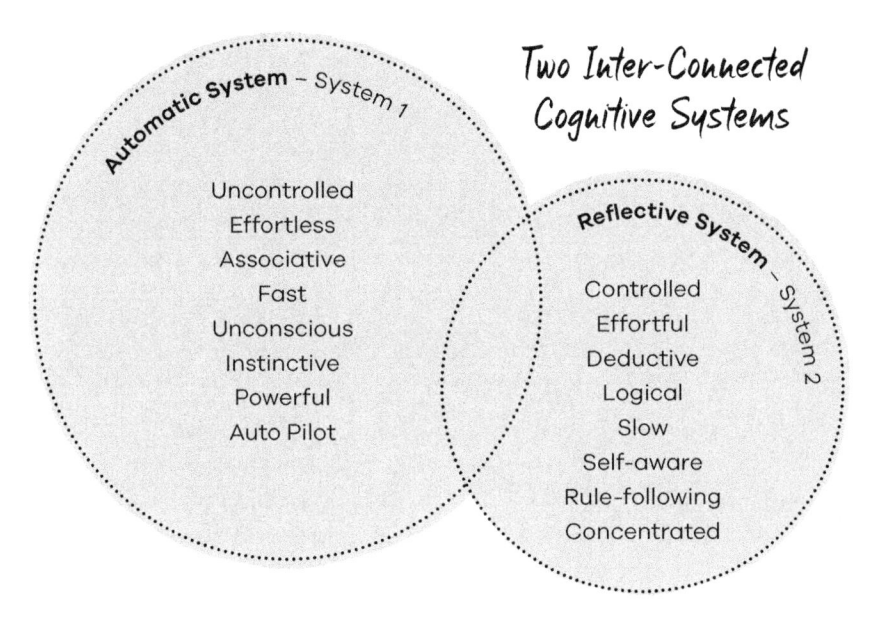

Two Inter-Connected Cognitive Systems

Automatic System – System 1
- Uncontrolled
- Effortless
- Associative
- Fast
- Unconscious
- Instinctive
- Powerful
- Auto Pilot

Reflective System – System 2
- Controlled
- Effortful
- Deductive
- Logical
- Slow
- Self-aware
- Rule-following
- Concentrated

Image created by Christina Hucke, Lisa Kepinski and Tinna C. Nielsen based on works by Thaler, Sunstein, Haidt, Kahneman, and others

The majority of what we do and the decisions we make are based on instinctive and emotional reactions in our automatic system 1. This is a fast system, making split-second judgements and reactions, that we do not control.

> The automatic system 1 is not really a system of **THINKING**, but more a system of **DOING**.

Whereas, system 2 is a conscious, self-reflective, slow and rational mode of thinking. In judgement and decision making, there is often a gap between system 1 and 2, thus between what we do and our intentions.

The unconscious mind (system 1) uses instinctive associations and mental shortcuts called cognitive biases to react fast and effortlessly, to process information, and make judgements. These are unreflective mental errors that can trigger thoughts, decisions, and behaviours in both negative and positive ways towards people, ideas, situations, language, objects, solutions, and more. We make a quick association between what we see or hear and a conclusion. If we have positive associations, we are more likely to process more of the information a person shares with us, or like their idea better, than when negative associations are triggered. This influences if we include or exclude them. For example, deciding who to call upon in a team meeting may be based on quick, unconscious perceptions of who we like and dislike and can come at the cost of ignoring people who may have valuable contributions.

> We are blind to the gap between our knowledge and intentions (system 2) to have all people in a team to speak up and contribute at their best, while having behaviours and actions (system 1) that result in only hearing from a few people and silencing others based on unconscious instincts, associations, biases, and social dynamics.

In situations of ambiguity, complexity, mental overload, and time pressure, we use the effortless and automatic mental processes to make judgements and conclusions even more. However, we rarely realise this is happening. As a result, we are often blind to the negative implications that biases have on our behaviours and decisions.

Two Inter-Connected Cognitive Systems

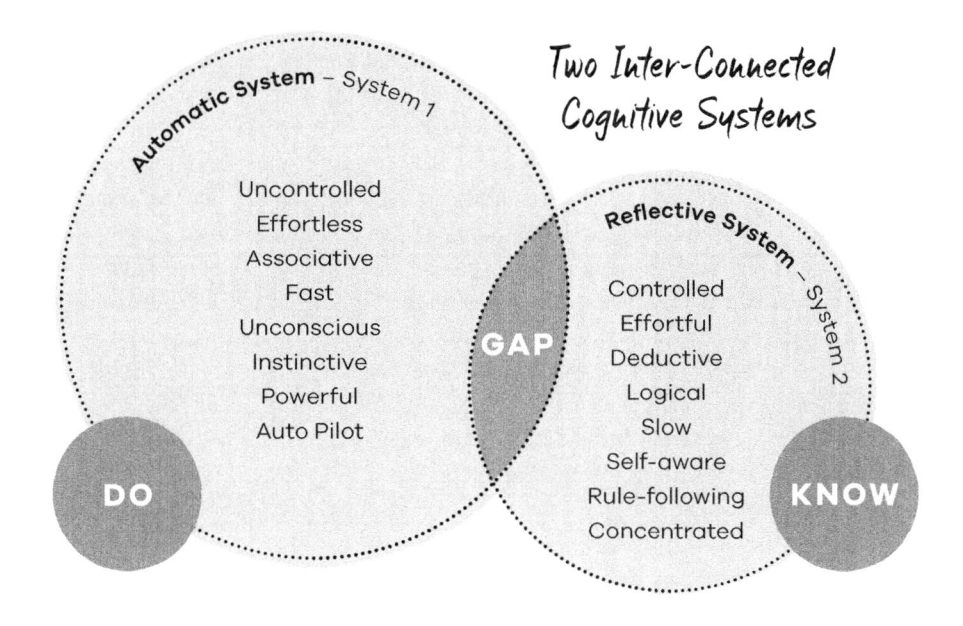

Automatic System – System 1
- Uncontrolled
- Effortless
- Associative
- Fast
- Unconscious
- Instinctive
- Powerful
- Auto Pilot

DO

GAP

Reflective System – System 2
- Controlled
- Effortful
- Deductive
- Logical
- Slow
- Self-aware
- Rule-following
- Concentrated

KNOW

Let's take a closer look at the effect of this gap and blind spots and unfold how these play out and manifest as an unintended and undesirable reality.

Absurd realities
Implications of our unconscious actions

A body of research, as well as evidence from organisations and communities worldwide, shows the implications of our unconscious actions and the resulting absurdities that play out and why it's so crucial that we change this now.

> As you read this, please stay optimistic.
> We have made sure that the 30 inclusive actions in this Action Guide empower you to change these and make inclusion the norm everywhere, for everyone.

Accent matters

Reality!

It takes us less than 30 seconds to linguistically profile a speaker and make quick decisions on their ethnic origin, socio-economic class, and backgrounds. Often these snap judgements are incorrect, but we still act upon them. We are more likely to be biased against people who have accents different to ours or are markers for 'undesirable characteristics' that we unconsciously attribute to certain accents. We assign values, such as pleasantness, prestige, and even intelligence, based on accent. Furthermore, most people (unconsciously) believe more in facts shared with us by a person who has the same accent as ourselves, than when those same facts are shared with us by a person with an unfamiliar accent.[10]

Absurd?

Surely no leader would rationally argue that an accent is the reason we buy-in on a great idea or not, nor would we rationally believe that people with the same accent as ourselves are the most competent. But in our behaviour, this is a reality and the implications are manifold. Absurd reality, isn't it?

Your actions?
→ Are you wondering about how your leadership is affected by the accents of the people you work with, interact with, or lead?
→ Are you wondering if you have been distracted by accents (such as thinking *"Where are they from?"*) rather than listening to what the person was saying?
→ Are you wondering if you have a pattern of more frequently calling upon native speakers of your own language?

Watch: "We stigmatize accents, but language belongs to everyone" by Hernan Diaz, Pultizer nominee & Associate Director of the Hispanic Institute at Columbia University
https://www.youtube.com/watch?v=xoOLBi8XL7I

Who says it matters

Reality!

Whose voice is heard is strongly influenced by mental associations. It's a socialised norm that its 'ok' to interrupt women more than men. Women are interrupted 2.8 times more than men in meetings. The interruptions are done by both men and women, showing that we all have internalised this absurd notion that its 'acceptable' to interrupt women. But the majority of interruptions come from men. And the reverse doesn't play out, as women rarely interrupt men. In meetings where men outnumber women, there is a 25% reduction in women's contributions. And if you are wondering if having a more senior leadership role would stop that, ... well, it doesn't. A study of U.S. female Supreme Court justices found that they were interrupted 30 times more than their fellow male judges. No matter the leadership level, women are still disproportionately interrupted, talked over, and have their ideas unacknowledged and picked up by their male colleagues without credit for the original idea. This pattern goes beyond gender, and also plays out at even higher rates with people who are in underrepresented groups.[11]

Absurd?

Would any leader believe that the best way to benefit from the knowledge and skills of the people they hired for the team, is for them to block each other from sharing and contributing fully? No? Well, that's what interruptions do, and unfortunately it's a norm rarely being stopped by leaders and team members. They don't even notice it happening. Absurd reality, isn't it?

Your actions?
→ Are you wondering who is not being heard in your meetings and on your team and who is being interrupted?
→ Are you wondering about your last meeting, and if you had an unintended pattern of interruptions of others?
→ What are opportunities you are missing out on as a result?

Want to see how your country averages against other country averages? See the free Global Report tool by Woman Interrupted at http://www.womaninterruptedapp.com/

Speaking first matters

Reality!
If a person with high authority opens a discussion with expressing their view first, then others can hold back from offering contrary important information. They go along with the prevailing view and perhaps incorrect information due to an unconscious belief that 'status' equates to the 'correct' view. The first people speaking up in a group will also influence the perception and engagement of the others in the group.[12]

Absurd?
Have you met leaders or project managers saying that they always speak first themselves or let the most powerful in the group speak first with the intention to make everyone else in the group contribute less, self-silence, or doubt their own view and thus not share it?

We haven't! But we have seen it play out in almost all teams again and again. And research supports this. Absurd reality, isn't it?

Your actions?
→ Are you wondering if you are getting access to the diversity of attributes and skills in the meetings you facilitate?
→ Are you wondering if you are missing out on new opportunities or wasting potential?
→ Are you wondering if by speaking first, you are perpetuating a hierarchical culture and maintaining inequality?

Recognising new ideas matters

Reality!

With profound shifts towards technology-based developments, artificial intelligence, robotics, and machine learning, there is still a strong demand and need for the human ability to think critically, be creative, and generate new ideas and problem solving. The foundation for this is leadership and cultures that support people sharing contrarian views, challenging the status quo, asking curious questions, questioning data, making suggestions for changes, and sharing new ideas. Surveys show that the majority of leaders know this is a MUST, but employees and citizens they don't always experience this. Research shows that leaders often say critical thinking is needed, but actively disregard employee concerns and ideas. There are several reasons for this, such as the unconscious mind preference for the familiar and status quo, as well as availability bias. This means that we don't seek out or recognise the 'new', and thus don't view it as relevant, competent, or important.[13]

Absurd?

Would a leader who knows the importance of agility, innovation, engagement, and inclusion rationality argue that it's smart to say *"critical thinking is needed"*, but then disregard new ideas or suggestions that employees or citizens put forth to challenge the status quo? Would they tell them, *"I only believe in new ideas that I recognise."*? Absurd reality, isn't it?

Your actions?

→ Are you wondering about how people in your team or community perceive your openness to hearing contrary ideas, and how you could turn this around?

→ Are you wondering if people feel supported to share 'new' thinking and speaking up to challenge the status quo?

How conducting idea generation matters

Reality!

Most idea generation sessions are spontaneous, open, verbal, highly active, and time-compressed. But this doesn't create the optimal conditions for idea generation from all people in the group. Often this leads to 'the loudest voice wins' competition. The focus becomes on the dominating personalities rather than the intent of getting a wide range of ideas. This format doesn't suit well the estimated 20-40% of people who are introverted. The difference is that introverts 'think-talk-think' while extroverted 'talk-think-talk'. Spontaneous verbal brainstorming not only can fit better for extroverted styles, but also with native language speakers, those who prefer big picture thinking over detailed process analysis, those from individualistic cultures rather than group harmonious cultures, and those who are in the majority group. Also, patterns of idea suppression develop with the early ideas expressed taking preference and shutting down new, different ideas being offered. And by approaching ideation to have an outcome of generating solutions has been shown to limit innovation as opposed to asking for *"What questions should we be considering on this topic?"*.[14]

Absurd?

Would a leader rest the outcome to a problem or search for a new solution to just a few loud voices or extroverts on the team out of a belief that's the best possible way to do it? Yet, the often-used brainstorming format and facilitation contribute to that happening and being the norm. Absurd reality, isn't it?

Your actions?

→ Are you wondering about how strong are your new proposals based on team ideation?
→ Are you wondering what ideas did you miss out on receiving due to the ideation format used?
→ Are you wondering who's input was not leveraged?

Skin colour matters

Reality!

People with a dark skin tone have less opportunities and experience discrimination in many countries. So much research and real experiences have proven this repeatedly. Biases damage Black and Brown people's access to education, health care, voting, jobs, promotion, housing, investment, justice, and more. To survive and thrive, people with dark skin tones are pressurised to create 'facades of conformity'. Conformity stems from trying to make it easier and more comfortable for the majority White people to accept Black and Brown people. Their reality is that the more like the majority, then the greater the opportunities. This shows up through hair straightened, names changed, 'whitewashing' resumes to mask racial/ethnicity or nationality identity and hiding personal addresses associated with racial/ethnic or immigrant neighbourhoods, altering styles of dress, changing language and accent, and more. This comes at a high cost to wellbeing, with greater isolation and solitude, feeling of under constant threat, denial of true identity, and a lack of psychological safety. It also takes a huge toll on the ability to fully contribute and perform. Even successful leaders with dark skin experience inequality in opportunities. They are disproportionately handed (by people of all skin colours) so-called 'glass cliff' assignments, which may offer nice rewards but carry a greater risk of failure.[15]

Absurd?

Would a professional leader have as a mission to make employees with a dark skin tone spend a large part of their mental bandwidth on making their skin colour vanish to fit in at work and be fine with the organisation only leveraging half of their talent and skills as a consequence? Would politicians and civic leaders want to damage their economies by maintaining poverty and injustice? No? It's an absurd reality then, isn't it?

Your actions?
- Are you wondering if you and the culture you create with your actions contribute to such 'facades of conformity' or 'glass cliffs'?
- Are you wondering if your actions are that of a leader who is contributing to combat discrimination?

Recent doing matters

Reality!
What happened most recently will influence how and what we remember over a longer period. If the most recent experience was positive, then that will have a positive spill-over effect on our perception of all the other things that happened. Or if the last experience was negative, then that can make us remember all the previous elements in that event or period as negative, even though we experienced them as positive at the time that they happened. These recency bias and memory bias also influence decision-making and assessments in investment, social welfare, future planning, innovation, and basically in all other contexts as well.

It has also been proven to impact on employee performance evaluations because we tend to assess the most recent episode in performance, while (unintentionally) ignoring all other work done over the full evaluation time. This skews the performance assessment comments and the resulting rating (and related compensation) and will have implications for the person's access to opportunities. When writing feedback and facts (for example, negative and positive impressions or implications) immediately after an occurrence, then this helps to mitigate the influence of this bias.

Absurd?
No professional leader wants to make evaluations and decisions based only on a fraction of the relevant information or data available. But it turns out, that's what we do on a regular basis when we have not designed our processes to make sure all elements are included. Absurd reality, isn't it?

Your actions?
→ Are you wondering what you may have forgotten about your team members' contributions over the past year?
→ Are you wondering about lost opportunities and flawed evaluations of performance because what happened most recently?
→ Are you wondering if one recent mistake influenced you to have an overall negative view – of yourself or others?

Easy names matter

Reality!

Names influence how we perceive people and connote some personality characteristics ranging from warmth and cheerfulness to morality. We form more positive impressions of people with easy-to-pronounce names than with difficult-to-pronounce names. An important real-world implication of the name-pronunciation effect is that people with easier-to-pronounce surnames occupy higher status positions. We promote people more quickly and we also vote for people with names that we find 'easier to pronounce' than those with 'difficult to say' names. We also believe more often statements from people with easier-to-pronounce names than names that we find challenging. This effect carries over to products and company names with those that are easy to say performing better with higher sales and in the stock market.[16]

Absurd?

Who would deliberately and rationally select people for work that we consider important based on how easy it is to say their name? No one, hopefully! But the problem is that the way the human mind has evolved, we prefer to engage in actions that are easy over effortful. Our default is the familiar over what is unusual to us. In this way, we end up with the unconscious and irrational mind dominating our behaviour. And thus, we chose people based on a name instead of merit or facts. Absurd reality, isn't it?

Your actions?
→ Are you wondering if you have de-selected the best qualified idea or person due to their name – without even knowing?
→ Are you wondering if your ability to pronounce names unintentionally influences you in your choices and interactions?

Who we see matters

Reality!

Seeing images of successful people that we can relate to and perceive as role models (similar to ourselves), influences our self-perception and self-belief in a positive direction. This is especially the case for women and for minorities. Pictures of successful strong women and people of minority backgrounds on the walls in buildings (offices, schools, community halls, government spaces, and more), on organisations' websites, in communications and marketing materials, on actual products when human images are used, and as screen savers have been proven to increase their performance and improve others' perception of them. Being exposed to such images (and real role models, of course) on a regular basis also influences our belief in the organisation and community as a place where people can feel and say *"I belong, and others believe in me!"*.

Absurd?

Think of the images that are portrayed in office lobbies and hallways, in community centres, schools, hospitals, in public spaces, on websites, in communications, or on computer screen savers. Not many would leave it up to chance what is displayed if they knew a picture could enhance their own talent and that of others (whom they would like to perform well). Or would they? Too often we do not act accordingly with our knowledge. Absurd reality, isn't it?

Your actions?
→ Are you wondering how the portraits on the walls are influencing performance or a sense of belonging?
→ What kind of role modelling are you projecting to your employees and community members?

WHAT absurd realities do I notice?

These unconscious actions and biases described above are just a small selection of the absurd realities that we all create with our actions and without having intentions to do so. These illustrations of the implications of how biases can de-rail our behaviour and cultures are a reminder of the importance of leading inclusively.

If you want to learn more about how you are influenced by mental shortcuts and unconscious associations, we recommend you to take some of the many Implicit Association Tests (IAT): https://implicit.harvard.edu/implicit/

But don't stop with the IAT. And don't get despondent in realising your biases. We all have these. Instead, use the insights you gained about your own quick associations to energise you in taking action to lead inclusively. You have 30 actions that you can do in this book.

It's the 'doing' that we need to focus most on to close the intention-action gap.

Exclusion is not diminishing
Perhaps you might be thinking, *"Surely, we humans are evolving and getting smarter. Surely, we are behaving more inclusively"*. Well, no.

Research shows that rather than diminishing, progress towards more equity and inclusion is very slow or stalled.[17] In many cases, exclusion is increasing. In the workplace, one large study found that 40% of U.S. employees felt excluded.[18] While another study across 4 countries found that discrimination was experienced or witnessed by 55% of U.K. employees, 43% of French employees, 37% of German employees, and 61% of U.S. employees. And across all 4 countries, half of the employees felt their organisations should take more action to increase inclusion, equity, and diversity.[19] This may have been partly driven by the need that 60% of staff feel that they must hide their differences (their diversity) at work.[20] These feelings of a lack of belonging, rejection, hiding, and being ignored[21] carry high costs on personal, organisational and societal levels, with lower engagement, productivity, innovation, societal stability, and advancements.[22] Declines in employee engagement alone can cost employers 34% of their annual salary.[23] With 62% of U.S. employees feeling disengaged,[24] a pattern of 'showing up, but checked out' prevails with serious impact on productivity, profitability, growth, and retention.

Inequality is one of the greatest threats to our future. A poll across 27 countries, revealed that while there was support for increased gender equality, there was still limited support for increased ethnic, religious, and racial diversity.[25] Gains in one area of inclusion, didn't transfer to other areas of humanity. And many studies have shown that even with expressed support for gender equality, it has not triggered the needed actions to achieve it, with an estimated 100 years before this will happen if the current pace of actions continues.[26] Across several countries during late Spring 2020, the demonstrations for racial equality showed citizens' lack of acceptance of a discriminating status quo. But concerningly, as the Global Social Mobility Index of 2020 shows, an overwhelming number of countries *are failing to provide the conditions in which their citizens can thrive, entrenching historical inequalities*.[27]

> "With the adoption of the 2030 Agenda for Sustainable Development, the international community pledged that no one would be left behind in the process of achieving sustainable development ... Those committing to this bold agenda recognized the threats to development progress that were already in place, including poverty; rising inequalities; disparities of opportunity, wealth and power; and global health threats. COVID-19 has amplified these threats and others, putting the development process further in peril, and risking pushing those who were already marginalized even further behind."
>
> **INTERNATIONAL LABOUR ORGANISATION (ILO)**
> *June 2020*[28]

Psychological stress, related to a feeling of a lack of autonomy and control in the face of uncertainty, exclusion from influence, and inequality is a shared global challenge according to the World Economic Forum's Global Risk reports in recent years. Not only does this have significant health consequences, it harms stability. Studies show that the psychological need for significance, as well as feeling included and having a sense of belonging to a group with a joint purpose and norms, when not met can then lead people to extremism to fulfill this emptiness. Polarisation is not driven by religion or ideology *per se*. Our fundamental human need for belonging will make people go to extremes to find groups and communities where this need can be potentially fulfilled.

Our (natural) tribal mentality and innate preference for homogeneity is being further strengthened by technology and social media, where algorithms create echo chambers of 'similar others' by recommending us to connect with people and groups based on similar interests and similar characteristics and identities. This also feeds us with suggestions for music, films, political views, media outlets, publications, and more. All of these are based on similarity with our existing preferences, tastes, opinions, and other gleaned 'facts' about us. At the same time, there is a strong tendency in the media to amplify the views of a small selected group of people in discussion platforms. And to also simplify views and facts with limiting implications for understanding, social cohesion and empathy, while strengthening the silencing of people. This is furthered with the polarisation of groups of people who interact within their own group rather than finding common bridges to other different groups of people. When we do not interact across differences, we do not train our mind to embrace and seek out difference and make use of diversity for the greater good of us all. Instead, we nurture the self-limiting human desire for homogeneity and similarity.

Making sure people are included, have a voice, feel listened to, and experience their insights and perspectives matter are not only important, they are crucial to our communities, workplaces, cities, organisations, and society.[29]

Many have called our current moment as the opportunity for a Great Reset to address the social injustices, and to do so with a social, economic, and moral dimension.[30]

> "The great challenge for all those who share leadership responsibilities is to respond to the crisis in a way that integrates the hopes of the future ... that respects the dignity and diversity of humankind."
>
> **KLAUS SCHWAB**
> **FOUNDER & EXECUTIVE CHAIR**
> **WORLD ECONOMIC FORUM**
> June 2020[31]

The time is now for leaders to emerge as courageous, inclusive leaders for reshaping our excluding and discriminatory absurd realities.

{ We are beyond inclusion being 'nice to have'. Inclusion is a global and local necessity. The need for leading inclusively and creating inclusive cultures is growing. }

The question is how to transform the current state to a more inclusive norm – everywhere, for everyone. And how, with your leadership, this can happen.

How we can change this

This nature of the human mind leaves us with a serious problem. What can we do? We cannot change and redesign how the human mind works. Knowing about our cognitive biases and the gap between the two systems in our mind, will not change how it influences us. Trying to be consciously aware of the unconscious is going to give us cognitive overload that will do the opposite of changing it. We cannot with willpower and good intentions in the rational mind change the automatic reactions in the unconscious mind.

What we can do instead, is to change and redesign the processes of how we collaborate, solve tasks, and make judgements and decisions. We can make sure that the way we interact with other people is inclusive, so our mind does not make snap judgements and negatively influences us to listen less or not process the information that is shared with us. We can make sure that the ways we facilitate meetings, idea-generate, collaborate, and make decisions in groups are designed to reduce group conformity and mitigate bias and self-silencing. We can make sure that what we do gives all people a voice and empowers them to perform at their best. We can make sure that selection processes are designed in ways that mitigate the influence of bias as the default. To achieve this, it requires that we all lead inclusively.

> This Action Guide is about doing exactly that. You get 30 examples of how you can make inclusion the norm in your leadership and make all processes inclusive by default.

To set the guiding frame, here is a model that we've created based on decades of working with leaders. It gives an overview of the many components of inclusive actions. This is what inclusive leaders, like you, can do.

The INCLUSIVE Action Model

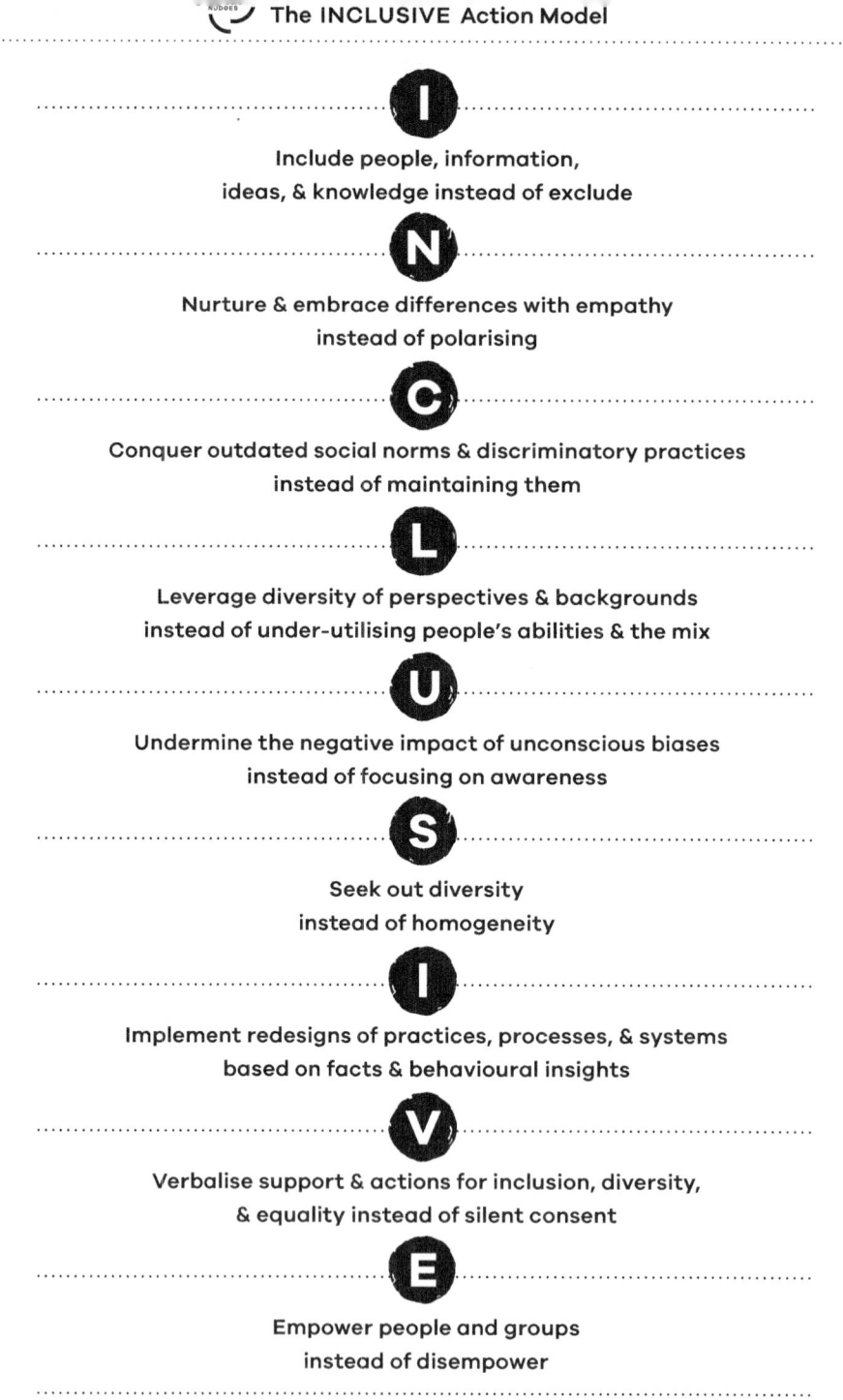

I
Include people, information,
ideas, & knowledge instead of exclude

N
Nurture & embrace differences with empathy
instead of polarising

C
Conquer outdated social norms & discriminatory practices
instead of maintaining them

L
Leverage diversity of perspectives & backgrounds
instead of under-utilising people's abilities & the mix

U
Undermine the negative impact of unconscious biases
instead of focusing on awareness

S
Seek out diversity
instead of homogeneity

I
Implement redesigns of practices, processes, & systems
based on facts & behavioural insights

V
Verbalise support & actions for inclusion, diversity,
& equality instead of silent consent

E
Empower people and groups
instead of disempower

The INCLUSIVE Action Model developed by Inclusion Nudges Founders, Tinna C. Nielsen & Lisa Kepinski, © 2020

Getting this right, pays off

Leaders in organisations who lead inclusively and create an inclusive culture in their teams see a rise in performance, better decision making, innovation, and collaboration, and they are 8 times more likely to achieve better outcomes.[32] So, the make-up of the team (diversity) and the way that the team works together (inclusion) are beyond being a *"nice to have"*. The same is true for inclusive communities where leaders empower people to be societal actors with a joint vision for their community and society. Civic participation and inclusive development have the potential of significantly improving society along multiple dimensions, such as health and economy, when done in ways that make people feel included, autonomous, empowered, and socially connected. Moreover, helping to shape the decisions that affect our own life and the lives of other people is fundamental to human well-being.[33] The benefits of inclusive organisations and societies at a larger scale are stability, higher transparency, lower corruption, a stronger rule of law, and higher trust in institutions and with each other.[34]

> "One hundred and seventy countries are going to finish this year [2020] with a smaller economy than at the start of the year, and we already project that there will be more debt, bigger deficits, and more unemployment. And there is a very high risk of more inequality and more poverty. Unless we act."
>
> **KRISTALINA GEORGIEVA,**
> **MANAGING DIRECTOR**
> **INTERNATIONAL MONETARY FUND**
> *3 June 2020*[35]

The call to action couldn't be more clear. What you do as a leader matters to our future. This Action Guide can help navigate you with some proven, concrete things that you can put in play right now.

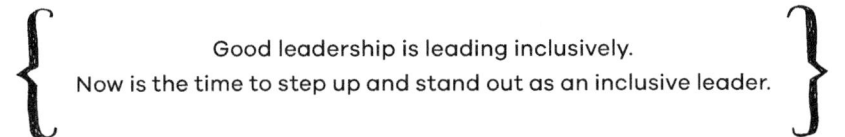

{ Good leadership is leading inclusively.
Now is the time to step up and stand out as an inclusive leader. }

The definitions we use

Diversity: The mix of all of us
Diversity is about people. This includes their demographic differences, backgrounds, multiple identities, and their unique experiences, perspectives, knowledge, abilities, ideas, and more. Diversity is not referencing specific characteristics of only 'the minority' within a group of people or in society. Diversity is referencing *all people and differences among us*. Diversity is the mix of all of us.

Equity: The fairness frame for the mix
Equity is about ensuring that all people have equal access to opportunities and fair treatment, and ensuring elimination of discriminatory practices, systems, laws, policies, social norms, and cultural traditions. Equity encompasses a balancing of power and correcting where inequality exists. It is also about patterns of behaviour and processes developed and used which may be continuing inequality. Within some contexts, equity may have a legal mandate attached to achieving it, along with penalties for not. The intent of equity is fairness to all.

Inclusion: Welcoming and applying the mix
Inclusion is focused on fostering the structure, system, processes, culture, behaviour, and mindset that embrace and respect all people and all our diversity. It embraces *all people*. Inclusion is about ensuring that diversity of knowledge, perspectives, information, and ideas are welcomed and being used. Inclusion is when we seek out diversity, when we challenge excluding norms and stereotypes, when we are open to others, and when we speak up. Inclusion is when all people are valued and able to participate and contribute to their fullest. Inclusion is welcoming and applying the mix of all of us.

Belonging: I feel valued as a part of the mix
Belonging focuses on the person's experience within a setting—they are welcomed, structures exist to ensure fairness, and they feel that they can be their full, authentic self within that culture, group, or setting. They don't have to cover who they are or downplay personal traits. As a result, they don't suffer the limiting toll this can bring. Belonging is when people feel seen and heard, feel they naturally belong to a group, feel safe, and feel valued. This results from having equitable and inclusive practices, norms, cultures, and systems. When diversity, equity, and inclusion are done well, then belonging results.

SECTION 2:

The Power of Inclusion Nudges

This is how you close the INTENTION-ACTION GAP and make the most of human potential and diversity

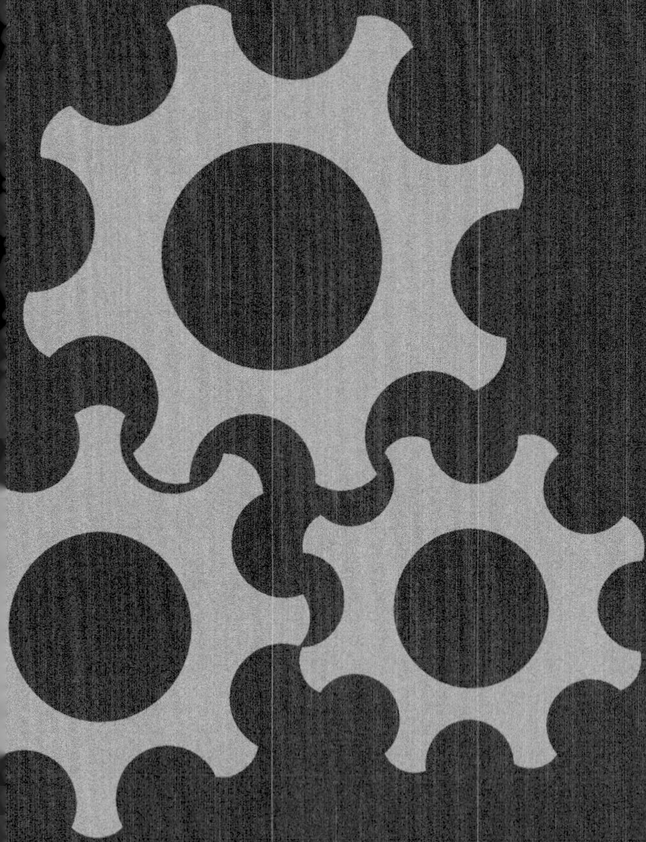

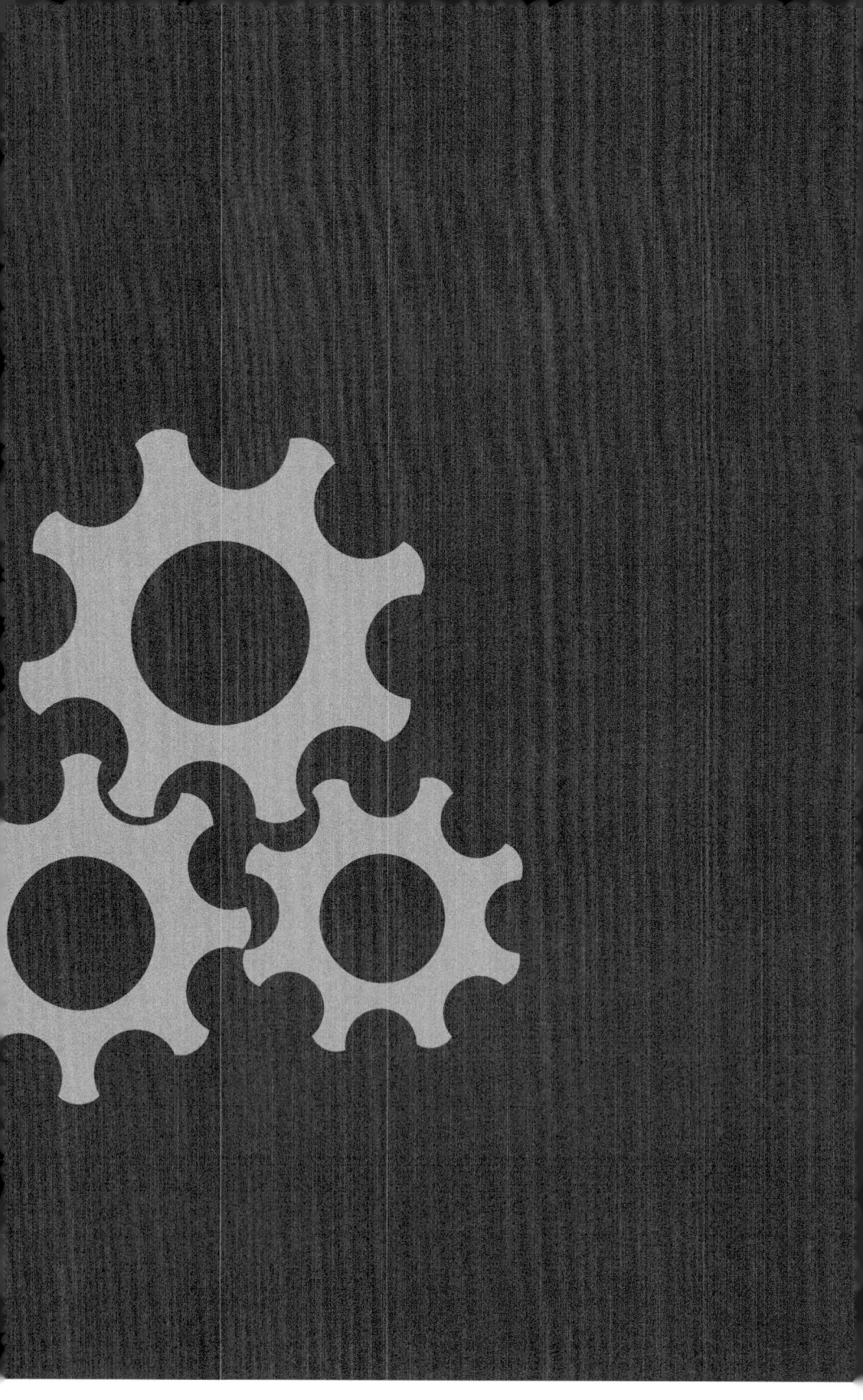

What is an Inclusion Nudge?

The inclusive actions in this Action Guide are grounded in the evidence-based change approach called Inclusion Nudges.

> An **INCLUSION NUDGE** is an action designed to influence the unconscious mind and make it easy to be inclusive and do inclusion automatically in daily actions.
>
> These actions are practical applications of basic insights about human behaviour and decision making (from behavioural and social sciences, nudge theory, as well as knowledge about the hidden barriers to achieve inclusion). These inclusive actions work because they nudge (steer) the unconscious mind (your own and that of others) to change behaviour to be inclusive in alignment with our knowledge about the importance of this and also in alignment with our own intentions to be great leaders.

The Inclusion Nudges change approach has three purposes and, thus, three types of designed actions that work – sometimes separately and sometimes together. These are described below.

Three types of Inclusion Nudges

→ **Process actions:** You can design processes to ensure the ability in yourself and in others to be and do inclusion automatically in daily actions. Research has identified that change comes from making it effortless to do the new behaviour. That's why it's crucial and effective to design processes (meeting facilitation, decision making, idea generation, innovation, promotions, hiring, strategy planning, and more) in ways that reduce the negative influence of bias and are inclusive of diverse perspectives by default. This is an effective way to engage people in making the culture in teams, communities, and organisations inclusive as the norm. We call these *Process Design* Inclusion Nudges.

→ **Motivational actions:** You visualise the hidden patterns and the implications of these both to yourself and to others to create motivation in the unconscious mind to be inclusive. You can get many people engaged in creating the changes without having to tell them to or convince them. Research has proven again and again that change happens when we see and feel the need for change (in the unconscious mind) and not when we rationally understand the need for change. We call these *Feel the Need* Inclusion Nudges.

→ **Framing actions:** You can change your own perceptions and split-second judgements, as well as those of other people by the words you use, the way you communicate, how you present a problem, issue, task, or set up the physical space. A body of research shows how our perceptions are influenced by hidden cues that trigger associations in our unconscious mind. When you change the cues, you can prime action, and change perceptions of diversity as a 'burden' to be a 'resource', you can mitigate and change negative stereotypes, perceptions, and also increase individual performance. We call these *Framing Perceptions* Inclusion Nudges.

The 30 actions in this book are a mix of these three types and we have selected them for their relevance to each of the **INCLUSIVE** Action model elements. This will make it easy for you to make sure you cover all the aspects of leading inclusively.

Thought leaders for a new approach

The Inclusion Nudges change approach was developed by the authors, Lisa Kepinski and Tinna C. Nielsen, in 2013 when we were both working as leaders with global responsibility for inclusion and diversity in multinationals—Lisa in France and Tinna in Denmark. We merged our change approaches and backgrounds in behavioural sciences, as well as our experience as leaders and change makers, and we developed the concept and coined the term 'Inclusion Nudges'. Today, Inclusion Nudges is internationally recognised as game changing and as a means to achieve inclusive outcomes effectively.

The Inclusion Nudges change approach is inspired by behavioural economics and the nudge theory created by Nobel Laurate Richard Thaler and Cass

Sunstein. Nudging is a technique that helps people change their behaviour without the need of convincing them with rational arguments, threats, or punishments. A nudge is choice architecture, where the environment, the system default, or the anchor of the thought process has been designed to help the unconscious mind automatically make a directed choice in a predictable direction.[36] The person does not think actively about the change nor do they need to engage their own willpower to alter behaviour. Thaler and Sunstein describe a good nudge as a behavioural intervention that is carried out to influence the choice and behaviour of people in accordance with their own interests or good intentions.

The power of nudging and Inclusion Nudges

Both nudging and Inclusion Nudges have these commonalities:

- Minimising the impact of mental shortcuts
- Not relying on the conscious mind to drive change
- Not using rational arguments to convince people to change
- Making the desired behaviour automatic
- Align behaviour with self-interest and intent
- Not using threats or punishment
- Respecting freedom of choice
- Mostly low cost or no cost
- Nudging for the greater good

The Inclusion Nudges change approach closes the gaps and makes it easy to do inclusiveness as the norm everywhere. And it's no longer the sole responsibility of the leader but a very inclusive development process with the people it's about.

In our own work as leaders, advisors, and change makers in many communities and organisations worldwide we, Tinna and Lisa, have seen first-hand the power of the Inclusion Nudges approach and how applying behavioural science insights promotes more inclusion as a means to strengthen:

leadership civil engagement belonging
empathy agility well-being unity creativity
equal opportunities applying all talents
business strategies collaboration product development
openness empowerment economy
engagement playfulness innovation
decision making performance
participatory co-creation public services

... and much more of what we need to thrive
collectively and individually

{ The most impactful about this approach is the potential of turning the barriers of the unconscious mind into strengths and levers for inclusive change, business, growth, and development. }

Intentional and inclusive choice architecture

Everything around us is *'choice architecture'* which is influencing our decisions and behaviour. We should make sure that our leadership, organisations, communities, policies, and society are actually designed with intentional choice architecture that will be good for people and will be inclusive. This was our motivation back in 2013 for merging our extensive knowledge about inclusion, diversity, and equality with nudge theory to create the Inclusion Nudges methodology and global initiative.

We published *The Inclusion Nudges Guidebook* (2020) with 100 examples to empower and enable as many people as possible to make inclusion the norm everywhere, for everyone.

This Action Guide contains 30 examples that have been specifically designed and selected for leaders. To get more inspiration and examples, we encourage you to read the full guidebook with all 100+ examples.

You can also read the other Action Guides, such as the *Action Guide for Talent Selection* and the *Action Guide for Motivating Allies*.

> Also, take a look at the Inclusion Nudges global initiative website for many more resources to support you leading inclusively.
> www.inclusion-nudges.org

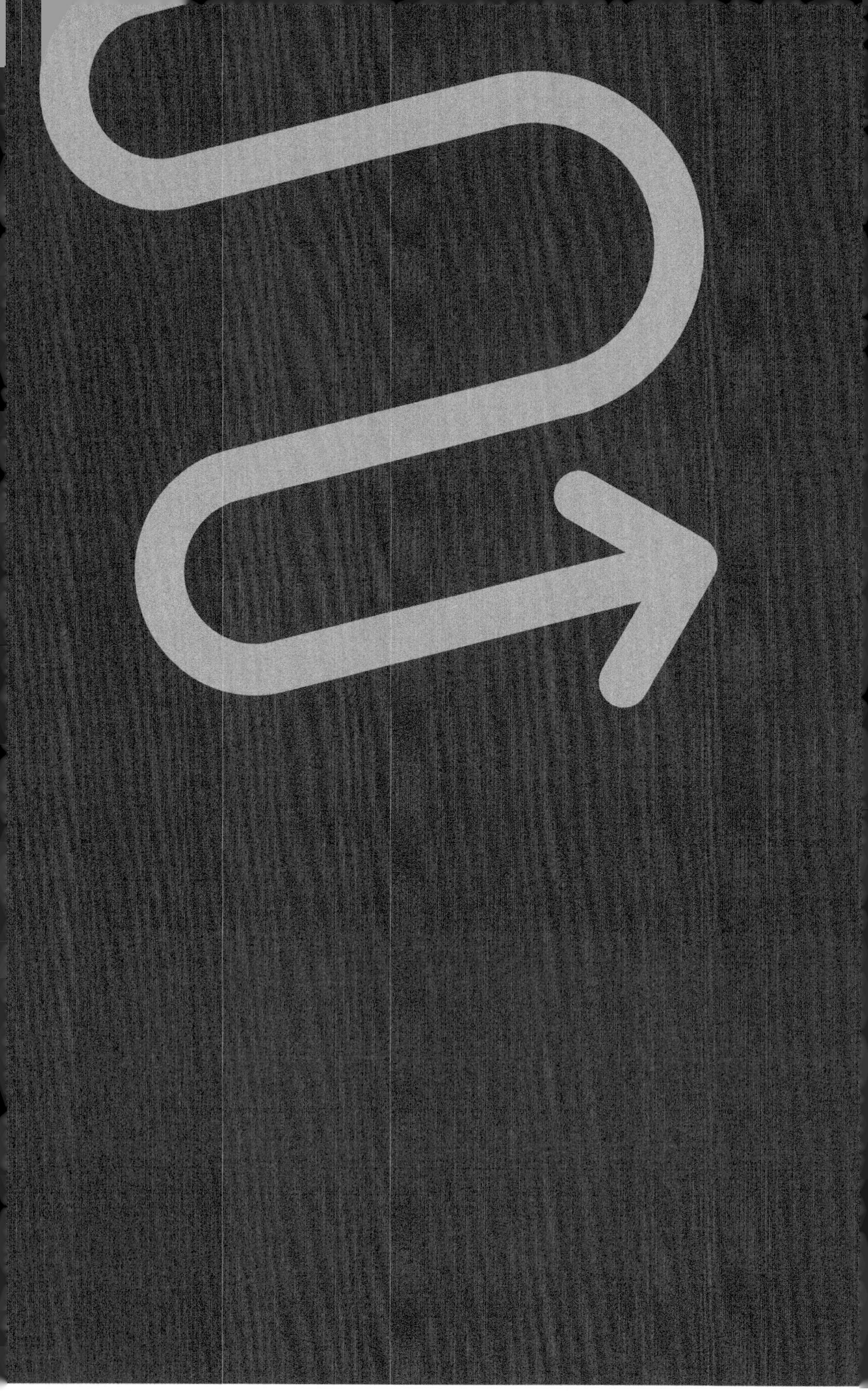

SECTION 3

Inclusive Actions for Leaders

> Action by action, I make inclusion the norm — everywhere, for everyone

How to use this Action Guide

This Action Guide offers you practical examples to be inclusive in your work to achieve better outcomes. These have designed by and written up step by step by the authors based on our years of work as leaders and with leaders in many organisations around the world and across a wide variety of sectors. Half the examples in this Action Guide come from the work of other leaders and change makers. All examples have been put into practice by many leaders around the world.

The examples will spark creativity in your mind when you start thinking about how you can apply these actions in your own context and leadership. So, when you come across an example from a completely different sector or setting than the one you work or live in, don't discount it. Read on. This might be the example that will make the biggest difference for you in terms of taking innovative action.

The actions have been mapped to the **INCLUSIVE** Action model, offering you 3 concrete things you can do to lead inclusively for each of the recommendations in the model. We have also offered some additional bonus examples that enable the optimal conditions for you to focus on these.

The Inclusion Nudges application principles

Oh, wow!
Be prepared for innovative thinking! These will probably feel different from how you've seen inclusion approached before. This approach requires thinking and acting as a change maker and innovator.

Be courageous!

Have a think!
You'll need to adapt the examples to your context. Explore what is the core of the challenge. Think about what are the stuck patterns in your work for inclusion.

Take a deeper look!

Give it a go!
Use the Inclusion Nudge examples and methodology to design interventions that can work in your context. It only makes a difference if you try it out. Test it and review it!

You can do this!

Share & be fair!
The authors and people sharing examples have donated their time and expertise for social change. The examples are shared to inspire, not for others to make money on.

Join us in sharing what works!

To see more about the Inclusion Nudges application principles, please refer to section 4.

The INCLUSIVE Action Model

I — Include people, information, ideas, & knowledge instead of exclude

N — Nurture & embrace differences with empathy instead of polarising

C — Conquer outdated social norms & discriminatory practices instead of maintaining them

L — Leverage diversity of perspectives & backgrounds instead of under-utilising people's abilities & the mix

U — Undermine the negative impact of unconscious biases instead of focusing on awareness

S — Seek out diversity instead of homogeneity

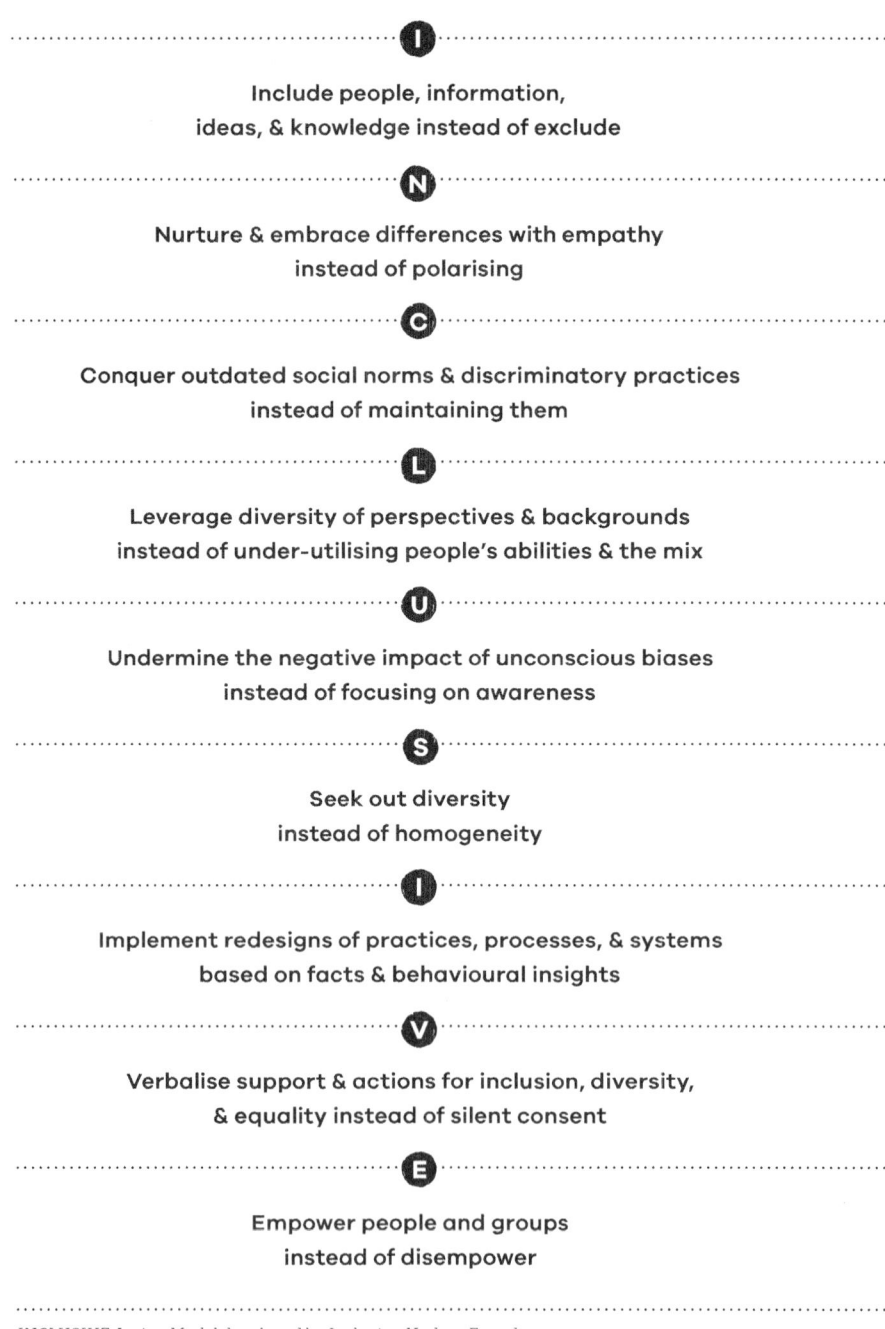

I — Implement redesigns of practices, processes, & systems based on facts & behavioural insights

V — Verbalise support & actions for inclusion, diversity, & equality instead of silent consent

E — Empower people and groups instead of disempower

INCLUSIVE Action Model developed by Inclusion Nudges Founders, Tinna C. Nielsen & Lisa Kepinski, © 2020

30 Inclusion Nudges

I
Write Before Talking to Reduce Group Conformity	55
Submit Anonymous Ideas Before Meeting	60
Reframe Mobility Question from Neutral to Inclusive	63

N
Prompters to Connect & Increase Belonging	70
Social Shuffle to Include Others	76
Physical Prompters to Interrupt Bias	83

C
'Flexible Work' as the Default in the Job Request Form	90
Interrupt Gender Caregiver Stereotype with Images	94
Experience Disability in Real Meetings	100

L
Start with 'Critical Thinking' Statement	104
Invite a 'Skills Pitch' from Everyone	107
Share with a Peer to Access Diversity in Groups	109

U
Ask Flip Questions to Change Your Perceptions in the Moment	114
Structured Scoring of 6 Qualifications	120
Colour Code People to Ensure Meritocracy	126

S
How Diverse Is Your Network Inner Circle?	132
Maximum 70% Homogeneity Team Composition & Target	138
Difference as Criterion for Selection, Not De-Selection	144

I
Anonymise People to Focus on Merit	148
Default as 'All Qualified' & 'Why Not'	155
Neutral Observer in Evaluation Meetings	159

V
'If Not, Why Not' Accountability	166
Show the Hidden People by Reversing the Numbers	171
Valuing Staff Contributions for Inclusive Culture	174

E
The Speech Bubble Intervention	178
Checklist to Balance In-Group & Out-Group Opportunities	189
How Diverse Is Your Universe	197

Bonus Actions!
Tech Free Meeting & Human Connection	204
Email Autoreply Releasing Time to Be Present	210
Simplify Accountability for Achieving Commitments & Goals	215

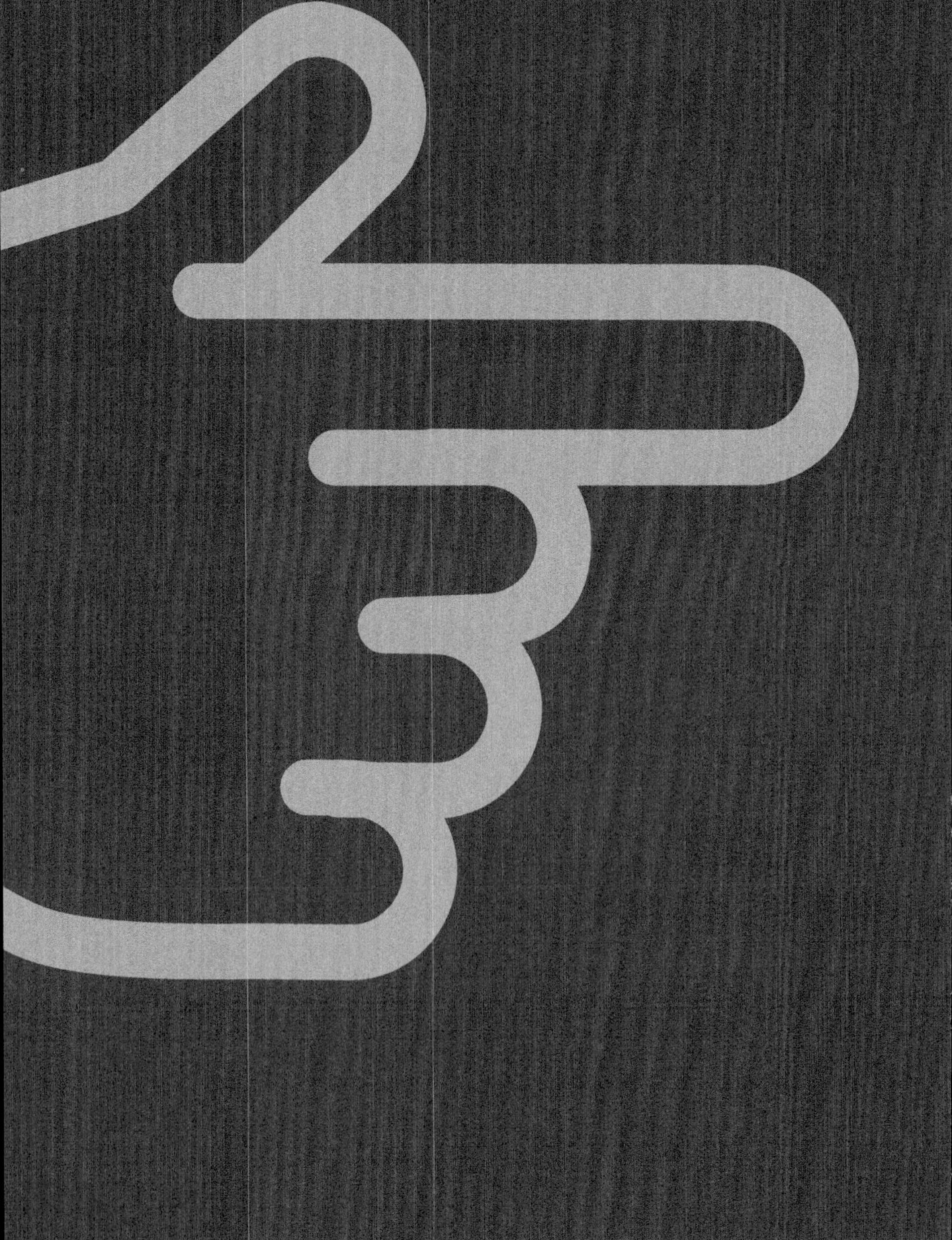

I N C L U S I V E

Include people, information,
ideas, & knowledge instead of exclude

Write Before Talking to Reduce Group Conformity

The Challenge

Group conformity and groupthink are barriers to leveraging a diversity of knowledge, perspectives, and ideas. Such group dynamics can prohibit that an inclusive culture develops regardless of the good intentions to use the full potential of all the people in a group. Often managers, facilitators, and project leaders encourage team members to share their points of view and perspectives or 'speak up'. How often have you heard as a way to get input in a work process or in a meeting, a leader say something like *'speak up'* or *'say something if you need to'* or *'tell me if I'm wrong'*. While the wishes are good, the process is problematic and may not yield the input of perspectives being sought. It is simply not enough to tell people to speak up.

This can become a case of the loudest gets heard. Another pitfall can be that leaders tend to support the ideas of those with whom they have some kind of affinity or those in their in-group. It is important to design the process to be inclusive by default. This is one simple way to do that.

The Inclusion Nudge

In facilitating collaboration in groups, instruct participants to write their perspective on notes (anonymous) before talking. All participants put the notes in a pile on the table/or stick to wall, and they take turn in picking up and reading out the notes to the group.

Purpose: Get access to diverse perspectives, reduce group conformity and leverage the diverse perspectives of the people in a group.

How To

Instead of asking people in a group to speak up or share their perspective verbally, make it an integrated part of the work process to write diverse perspective on paper (anonymously).

This may be in meetings, trainings, decision-making processes, discussions, talent review processes, and anywhere in which receiving input from all is needed for better outcomes.

Lisa Kepinski, Founder of Inclusion Institute, and **Tinna C. Nielsen,** Founder of Move the Elephant for Inclusiveness, have used this design for years with many leaders. In one of Tinna's organisations, it was part of a leadership program on inclusive leadership and team development.

❶ Introduction
Show managers and teams a film clip of the Solomon Asch experiments to illustrate the power of conformity. Inform them that 1/3 conform.[37] Ask the participants to share how this is playing out in their own group or in those they lead or participate in.

❷ Inform
Inform the participants that our good intentions to verbally encourage each other to speak up and share our views, even when we do not agree, is not enough to stop group conformity and self-silencing. What is lost is access to and the ability to leverage the diversity of perspectives from the group which are important to apply in task-solving processes and decision-making processes to improve solutions, performance, and innovation.[38]

❸ Write before talking
Share this practical example of how easily this can be changed. Tell the participants that all they have to do when facilitating meetings, collaborating, making decisions in groups, is to instruct people to write before they talk. This can be done in multiple variations:

- → Write your most critical inner voice
- → Write your perspective on this challenge
- → Write your pro and con arguments
- → Write your biggest worry
- → Write your suggestion for a solution

❹ Share diverse perspectives in plenary

Next, all notes are placed in a pile on the table (or in a box or hat or the wall) and the team members take turn in reading the notes out loud. They randomly pick notes, but not their own.

❺ Leverage diversity

Team members elaborate on each other's contributions, if necessary. This can also be facilitated by instructing all team members to find one or more argument(s) that supports or opposes a perspective contribution.

❻ Ensure decision alignment

Make a silent sense check of the decision. Having made a decision, ask all participants to write down what they understand has just been decided. This should be anonymous. Ask one person to read all the notes out loud. Often, the content turns out to be understood differently by the group members. Always allow extra time for a decision-making process to make sure everyone is aligned and has understood the same thing. And even better, make sure they commit to actions.

Alternative version: Share with a peer

In some situations, it might not be possible to write on notes, or you know that the people involved do not feel comfortable or able to write. Instead, you can use another variation of this design.

Read **SHARE WITH A PEER TO ACCESS DIVERSITY IN GROUPS** (→ page 109).

💻 Online design version

Make sure to also apply this design when you have online meetings. You will have to make sure that the chat function in the virtual platform you use can anonymise the participants. If that is not possible, instruct the participants to send their input to you in an email and you read these out loud to the group and invite them to discuss these diverse perspectives and insights. If you use the 'share with a peer' version get guidance on how to adjust to online meetings on page 110.

Impact

This simple process design gives access to diverse information, ideas, and knowledge by creating psychological safety for all people to share what's on their mind. All people are automatically being included. By making this part of the facilitation, it signals that the input of all is wanted and important.

With the thousands of leaders we, Tinna and Lisa, have worked with other the years, these ways of facilitating group collaboration is now applied by most of them across all functions, levels, sectors. We know executive teams do it, leaders in factories use it as part of **LEAN** board meetings, we see investors apply it in pitching sessions, and recruiters facilitate talent discussions this way. It is such a small change in something leaders already do, and it has such an immediate and large impact.

Authors' Comments & Behavioural Insights

This simple Inclusion Nudge (in multiple versions) is an impactful way to make inclusion in groups the norm without having to talk about inclusion. Making sure to get access to diverse perspectives and be inclusive of these, is the default way of facilitating when applying this kind of process design. This way the intention-action gap is diminished. We automatically include instead of exclude.

Why it works: behavioural insights

As outlined in the beginning of this Action Guide, group dynamics such as group conformity and groupthink have a big influence on people, collaboration, and outcomes. Without intention, we exclude and we conform. Psychological safety is one of the reasons it works to write before talking or tell a peer before sharing in plenary. This is a condition in which human beings feel safe to speak up, safe to learn, safe to contribute, and safe to challenge the status quo without fear of being embarrassed, marginalised, or sanctioned in any way.[39] Psychological safety is also a shared belief that the team is safe for interpersonal risk taking[40]. It all comes down to being able to show and employ one's self without fear of negative consequences of self-image, status, or career.[41]

These simple process designs foster an inclusive and psychological safe group culture, thus support wellbeing, engagement, and innovation. What's not to like?

INCLUSIVE

Include people, information,
ideas, & knowledge instead of exclude

Submit Anonymous Ideas Before Meeting

The Challenge

Dan Robertson, the director of Vercida Consulting, shares this process design to nudge for inclusive decision making by capitalising on **anonymous idea submissions.**

> **The Inclusion Nudge**
>
> Submit anonymous ideas before meeting.
> Discuss each idea based on merit and potential in the meeting.
> All team members vote.

Purpose: Receive diverse input from all people in the team (and potentially others) to improve the quality of evaluation and decision making.

How To

❶ Submit
Before a team meeting (in-person or virtual), participants submit their ideas for discussion anonymously. These are sent to the team administrator who simply codes these ideas using an A–Z scale.

❷ Review
In the team meeting, ideas are presented on a screen in the order in which they were submitted. The rules state that leaders and other participants

should refrain from asking whose idea it is, and instead they should simply focus on the merit of the idea itself.

❸ Discuss & vote
Debate the merit of each idea in turn and at the end of the meeting, vote, using a simple voting app. All votes must be anonymous to ensure voting decisions are not influenced by peer pressure or conformity bias.

When doing the voting in online meetings, you can use the poll function (if the platform has that feature). It's a great way to ensure anonymous voting and immediately see the results.

❹ Take it forward
Once the voting has been completed, the top 3 ideas are then taken to the next stage of decision-making.

❺ Multiple inclusive devil's advocate
This process can also be supplemented with a so-called Inclusive Devil's Advocate. One person in the group has the role of critiquing the project idea from an *inclusion lens*. Once a problem is found the role of the devil's advocate is to find a positive alternative to the idea being challenged.

Do this before the implementation of any new policy or programme – this could be anything from a new marketing strategy, a customer engagement project, a new approach to candidate hiring or job evaluations.

Whilst the term devil's advocate implies one single stakeholder, the process actually involves multiple stakeholders from many diverse groups. The idea goes out to a pool of devil's advocates. These individuals represent diverse stakeholders and may be part of an organisation's affinity groups.

The devil advocates self-nominate to be part of the 'devil's advocate' team to avoid any built-in favouritism.

The role of these different organisational stakeholders is to critically, but professionally, 'pull apart' the suggested idea and edit, amend, or change the idea, and to come with alternative but practical suggestions. Any new suggestion should be operational with the stated budget constraints and with the central criteria being one of total inclusion.

Once the original idea has been amended these are presented back to the project team. Part of the 'contract' of this process is the automatic adoption of any new suggestion unless it breaks budget constraints or a conflicting policy. Using an auto-adoption approach restricts room for negotiation and ensures the ideas of diverse stakeholders are included within the implementation stage.

Impact

The impact that Dan has seen are the risk of **groupthink** and **conforming bias** are greatly reduced, with ideas becoming more innovative through the utilisation of diverse stakeholders. Women and minority ethnic participants, in particular, reported greater confidence in the organisational decision-making process and are, thus, more likely to positively engage in future decision-making processes.

Authors' Comments & Behavioural Insights

Why it works: behavioural insights

This simple design nudges the unconscious mind to focus less on conforming to the view of others, and more on the content of the ideas. Biases, such as personal biases, affinity bias, and the **Ostrich Effect** (a bias that leads to avoiding information perceived as potentially unpleasant) are mitigated by actively inviting constructive critique of new ideas at the inception stage. The process also helps to reduce the influence of **in-group** and **out-group** on decision making by greatly improving the opportunity for all people to propose ideas. This process design makes it easy to include diverse information, ideas, and knowledge instead of exclude.

Publicly Available Resources

See this free tool for generating ideas, debiasing information gathering, and decision making, called **Candor** was developed by Professor **Loran Nordgren** of the Kellogg School of Management. It works because it decouples the generation of ideas from the evaluation of ideas and helps to avoid the problems of **idea anchoring** and **clustering.** https://usecandor.com/

Include people, information,
ideas, & knowledge instead of exclude

Reframe Mobility Question from Neutral to Inclusive

The Challenge

In many organisations, significantly more men than women receive international assignments, which are seen as a required career experience for promotion to senior roles. This explicit requirement, assignment pattern, and implicit norms sharply narrows the pipeline of internal women for senior executive roles. There is a need to widen this pipeline to be more gender balanced (and for many organisations to be more diverse in other ways, as well).

However, some questions, which are assumed to be neutral in design, are actually generating responses that indicate the questions are not as open and fair as assumed. For example, with a question about international mobility in an organisation, where **Lisa Kepinski,** Founder of Inclusion Institute, previously worked, a majority of the women opted out of international assignments as a career option, while a majority of the men over-opted in. More men responded favourably than actually would take an international assignment if presented one. The result was that the question response pool was not valid. It was not producing the same perspective taking in men and women as they considered the question. This 'neutral' question actually was a barrier to the organisation's goals of a diverse talent pipeline for new assignments and promotions. This is what Lisa did to change the status quo.

> ## The Inclusion Nudge
>
> Change a seemingly neutral question about international mobility to an inclusive question.
>
> The question in the talent process was changed from:
> "Are you internationally mobile?"
>
> To this question:
> "Would you consider an international assignment at some point in the future?"

Purpose: Reframe and redesign the question to shift perceptions to be more inclusive of diverse orientations of all people and to build a wider talent pipeline for future opportunities. This framing changes the anchor of the thought process, and thus changes the answer to the question.

How To

In the organisation where this *Framing Perception*Inclusion Nudge was designed, when filling in personal profiles in the talent management system, significantly more men than women answered *"yes"* to the question *"Are you internationally mobile?"*

This was a problem because answering *"no"* would have negative implications for career options and was a loss of good talents to enable the success of the organisation in other countries. Here's how this challenge was addressed.

❶ Analysis
Conduct extensive organisational research to reveal patterns of potential gender bias in the employee life cycle and organisational culture. Look for what Human Resource data reveals – where do the numbers change?

Results from this example's organisational assessment showed the gender gap in who had international assignments. A deeper look showed that the first-choice moment for an international assignment rested with the employee's answer to one question in their online talent profile. The question was *"Are you internationally mobile?"*

Lisa conducted interviews and focus groups to understand from which perspectives the question was being answered by people. And also, to explore if there is a mismatch with what the numbers show and actual aspirations.

She found that women tended to answer *"no"* due to reflection about the current moment, especially thoughts of home and life demands *("How will I ever get everything arranged? So much is depending on me to be here and available.")*. They answered from a **present orientation.** Men, however, tended to answer *"yes"* (*"I'll sort it out when the time comes. There's no firm offer right now."*). They answered from a **future orientation.** She also found that the number of women answering *"yes"* did not match the much larger number of women who said in the audit discussions that they actually would like to have an international career.

A further challenge was that the phrase of *'internationally mobile'* often was perceived by the women as a total relocation (as an all-or-nothing situation), which meant broader consequences for the employees and their family. However, the reality of the international assignment offer was that of a temporary situation with variable time frames and different living situations. So, the question itself was not aligned with the true intended outcome of building a talent pipeline for international work which entailed many different forms.

❷ Design
The design goal was to align with your intention of being inclusive of all. Lisa's organisation did this by changing the question with the purpose of framing it to be as neutral as possible and to instead get people to answer from the same orientation (present/future). The *Framing Perception* Inclusion Nudge put in place in this organisation was to change the question to be,

"Would you consider an international assignment at some point in the future?"

❸ Verify
Test the question on a wide range of diverse staff before implementing. Test various ways of framing the question to make sure you implement the most inclusive framing.

Impact

By simply reframing one question, more women (more than a 25 % increase in one year) said they would consider an international assignment. It's not that 25 % more women were all of a sudden internationally mobile, but that 25 % more women answered yes, due to a change in perception of the implications of answering yes. It can be assumed that in this case women answered the original question from a present frame of reference, thinking about the consequences on their private lives, and thus, being more reluctant. Whereas, men would answer from a future frame of reference, thinking this could work out when there is an actual offer later on. And it can also be assumed that men would answer *"yes"* based on insights that being registered as internationally mobile would further their career opportunities (which is in alignment with men applying to jobs when they master about 60 % of the required skills and women when mastering 100 %).

Lisa shares that one of the biggest obstacles to overcome in making this change was from the IT department that said the number of characters in the new question were too many for the space in the online talent management system. It wasn't that the IT colleagues didn't get the need for the change to happen or that they didn't have the skills to do it. It was that they didn't feel empowered to incur the expense to make the change to the online talent platform.

This involved another level of analysis to accomplish the change from this Inclusion Nudge. Lisa flipped her own perception of seeing resistance *("IT won't do this!")* to one of collaboration *("Who is the client of IT that can request this change to happen and enable IT to become a change partner in this redesign?")*. That perspective helped to identify who else needed to be engaged in the change process and to authorise the needed IT redesign work to complete this Inclusion Nudge implementation.

Authors' Comments & Behavioural Insights

This Inclusion Nudge was designed by Lisa when she worked as an internal inclusion and diversity leader in a multinational corporation, but reframing a seemingly neutral question like this, is applicable in all organisations because they will all be fighting for skilled talent in a global workforce. One critical trend in the labour market is an increased demand for highly skilled workers and a shortage in the future. This means that also organisations with a domestic orientation will need to make themselves attractive to skilled talent across borders. Questions like *"Would you be agile to work on international assignments for short periods of time?"* or *"Would you consider commuting to work in various locations?"* could be relevant. We recommend that you experiment with the powerful technique of reframing seemingly neutral questions to be inclusive in as many organisational areas as possible.

With this Inclusion Nudge example, the challenge is to better achieve a wide pool of employees who are actually open to international assignments. Many organisations can get stuck if they take an approach of blaming the women (or other diverse people that they are seeking to increase). This is usually automatically driven by stereotypes and established norms. It can be easier to think that the problem lies with the person, rather than with the organisation's own systems, cultural patterns, and decisions. Consider comments such as these below.

"Well, these women just don't want to leave their current homes."
"These women are not ambitious enough for such stretch assignments."
"These women lack the confidence for international leadership."

When these are expressed, then the opportunity to change the pattern is misdirected and lost is the leveraging of a wider source of talent.

However, for organisations that want to de-bias their systems, the starting point is with the actual decision moment. This is called **choice architecture** in behavioural economics terms. For this case of the international assignment talent pool, the de-biasing design process was to look at the actual question itself. Why were more men responding positively to the question, and why were more women responding negatively to the question? Deeper analysis revealed that men and women did not perceive the question in the same way. Research also shows that words appeal differently to men and women, and to people with other types of differences (such as nationality, age group, and others).

Why it works: behavioural insights

Having the same frame of reference to get the most accurate responses to questions is critical to produce accurate results. In this example, the **anchoring of perspective** of the time frame of *present* versus *future* was a variable in people's experience of the question. The way the original question was composed, it simply did not provide enough context to frame to the same view of what was being asked. An inclusive reference point is important in question design. Because we can all fall prey to biases influencing our question designs, we should seek out ways to hear others' views on the question before its implemented.

Though this is a *Framing Perceptions* Inclusion Nudge that shifts the perceptive of the question, it is also a *Process Design* Inclusion Nudge when it is implemented within the talent management process when designed in the IT talent system. It also could be used to support other process design changes, such as the way international assignments are designed, the communication of opportunities, and the selection process from the talent pool. The three types of Inclusion Nudges often have an integrated effect to all support wider organisational change initiatives. To get started, analysis should be conducted to reveal where is the most **critical challenge point** and start there.

This is a case of showing what is often described in nudge theory as the **"power of the small"**. The actual example in this case is seemingly of a small and simple change of rewording one question. But the level of research and analysis behind it, the time and engagement of others, and the measuring and testing were all actually quite intensive work. But the power of this small change (nudge) can have a big impact on the employees' career opportunities and organisation's success. This illustrates the importance designing to avoid that people exclude themselves from opportunities. It's an example of how we as leaders can make sure we include people, information, ideas, and knowledge instead of excluding. It's as simple as asking a question and collecting information about people.

INCLUSIVE

> **WHAT & HOW**
> I'll make sure to include people, information, ideas, & knowledge instead of exclude

I N C L U S I V E

Nurture & embrace differences with empathy instead of polarising

Prompters to Connect & Increase Belonging

The Challenge

Even with the best of intentions, it can be tricky to foster an inclusive culture and environment. We need to asses, design, and nudge ourselves to make inclusion happen rather than hoping that it will be on the top of our mind. In busy lives, cities, and workplace, we can often forget that we as humans have an innate need for social connection, happiness, and love.[42] When there is lower connection and less sense of belonging, research shows lower productivity, engagement, and retention. Social isolation can also have an impact on our health, which is equivalent to smoking 15 cigarettes a day.[43] We are happier when we connect with other people.[44]

In our workplaces, when we do connect at work it is through team meetings, events, and at the common food areas. But the normative pattern in most organisations is a preference of work tasks over social connection. We miss out on the important need for us to build connections with each other to increase trust and understanding beyond the superficial level. In cities, we use the space to transit, and forget the value of random meetings and our innate need to use our senses to feel connection to nature and the people around us.

Using 'prompter' can make it easier to meet, talk, and learn more about each other as an integrated part of city and workplace gatherings, events, conferences, and lunch breaks. These facilitate connection and understanding about each other, which is at the heart of inclusion and belonging. Below, we give examples of very different ways to do this.

The Inclusion Nudge

Use prompters to make it easier for people to interact and connect as an integrated part of work and events
(see examples below)

Purpose: Facilitate an inclusive environment of trust, connection, and familiarity by prompting the unconscious mind to change behaviour, which increases a sense of belonging as an integrated part of living and working.

How To

Here are several ways to enable social connection within meetings and events with some simple prompters.

Version 1: Prompt new conversations with buttons

At a public conference in 2018 and 2019, near the check-in area where participants received their conference badge, there was also a *"Diversity and Inclusion button station,"* shares **Chloe Sesta Jacobs**, Head of People and Culture (APAC) at Deputy (see her photos below).[45]

Photos by Chloe Sesta Jacob

The diversity and inclusion buttons covered many topics. Attendees could also write their own. She shared that through the button station, the conference hosts were encouraging attendees to embrace vulnerability and sharing as a strength. The badges enabled caring and respectful conversations about one's identity with other attendees. The buttons showed that appearances aren't always as they seemed, and led to many deep discussions between people.

Version 2: Prompt with story of your name

Lisa Kepinski, Founder of Inclusion Institute, and **Tinna C. Nielsen,** Founder of Move the Elephant for Inclusiveness, like an opener to introduce and more deeply connect people that is called **The Story of Your Name**. We first came across this over 15 years ago, used by a colleague, **Elaine Yarbrough** ✊, in a workshop. It has since been used by both of the authors, and undoubtedly many others, and was even recently cited in an article in the New York Times.[46] In the beginning of a meeting or workshop, we use this as a way to do introductions and learn more about each other. Each person is in control of their own story as they decide what they want to share and not share. Typically, the facilitator(s) starts it off with their own story of their name to create openness by sharing first and to model how to do it. Each story is personal. It may bring up naming traditions, cultural trends, history of immigration, pronunciations, special people they were named after, religious rules, ownership of their name, emotions, and more. Through this, we learn about the person and their self-identity. We remember them in a different way. One's name is something that is always in the workplace, yet we've rarely taken the time to find out more beyond the name and understand who are the people that we work with and what is their story. Adding The Story of Your Name to meetings and group work can be a very powerful way to deepen connection and create a more inclusive environment which can benefit the functioning of the team and its work.

Version 3: Prompt to reduce isolation with special tables

In one of Lisa's former workplaces, she noticed that most of the new interns (who were from diverse backgrounds) were each sitting separately and eating lunch alone in the canteen. Loneliness at work is hard enough, and this is compounded even more when you are also feeling acutely that you don't 'fit in' with the majority of employees around you. The toll on the person is deep. It can also impact how they feel about the organisation and ultimately if they would accept an offer of employment at the end of their internship.

So, she created a table designed for people eating without lunch partners. The interns loved the idea and they named it "The Single's Table".

Version 4: Prompt connection through common food area

Often organisations have open space offices. There are several reasons for this, with one being to foster greater connection across employees and to increase productivity and collaboration. However, many research studies are showing that the actual impact of open space office plans is leading to greater social isolation with staff wearing noise cancelling headphones or listening to music in order to reduce external distractions around them. Face-to-face interaction is reduced to about 70 %, while email messages increased by 50 %.[47] And job satisfaction and well-being decreased and absenteeism increased.[48] There was less social contact. However, there can be ways to facilitate **(design physical prompters)** connection. One organisation found that by having just one or two main coffee and food stations, rather than many smaller ones throughout the building, increased the occurrence of interaction with work colleagues. By having fewer and more centrally located refreshment areas, this brought a wider range of staff together. Not only did interaction increase, business performance also increased.[49]

Impact

Chloe shares that the identity badges at the conference created openings for having conversations with new people, especially in a large conference setting where it can feel isolating and people may not talk with each other at all. She said that many people *"were actually proud to share things about themselves which they may not have necessarily shared with others without these badges."*

Tinna and **Lisa** have seen how "The Story of Your Name" deepens connection across meeting participants in unexpected ways. They learn more about each other and this opens new conversations that lead to more sharing of diverse perspectives and input.

The Single's Table in **Lisa's** example became very popular with many regular employees as well as with the interns. A lot of regular staff said that they stayed away from eating in the canteen because they didn't want to sit alone amidst the crowds of people who had someone to sit with, so they just took their food back to their work desks. In the end, more tables like this were created in the canteen and it became easier to connect with work colleagues. The concept was expanded to other offices in this multinational with each local office deciding what to call the table that would prompt others to join in within their context.

Authors' Comments & Behavioural Insight

Why it works: behavioural insights

We are all influenced by social norms, which are unwritten rules of behaviour that are considered acceptable in a group or society. **Social norms** function to provide order and predictability. Because we all have a basic innate need to belong to social groups, we blindly follow the social norms and what the majority of people do. And those who do not follow the norms will suffer disapproval or may even be outcast from the group. Changing social norms can be difficult. Sometimes, a little help is needed to get more people to join in to make a change happen. This means that it's not just up to you to do it. We all know how difficult it can be to greet someone in the hallway if the norm is that nobody does that. If nobody shares anything personal about themselves, it's really not easy to start telling about your weekend or that your are in a difficult situation or other things that allows you to be your whole self and fully present with others at work, at events, in your community, etc.

The use of **prompters** can be very useful in shifting these strong social norms and hidden patterns. Prompters work as a means to achieving a desired outcome for all people in workplaces and groups – more meaningful connections and an increase of a sense of belonging.

Prompters are a mechanism designed to make it easier to do inclusiveness and alleviate our busy brains from having to remember to do something. Making time to talk and listen to each other the organisation and community benefits through increased connection that strengthens collaboration, productivity, retention, and more. However, it is important not to have this perceived as something extra, optional, or of low value.

Design these **connection prompters** to be a regular part of how meetings and events are conducted and how workplaces and public spaces in cities are designed. Let's be aware that any design of a physical space prompts behaviour in a certain way, so let's be more conscious and inclusive of how to do this. Connecting as human beings is the foundation of nurturing and embracing differences with empathy, which is one of the key behaviours in the Inclusion Nudges INCLUSIVE Action Model.

Publicly Available Resources

The **New York Times** has created a free online tool with their photos called **Picture Prompts** that is part of their educational resource called **The Learning Network** (freely available). While it is designed as a way to use a photo along with some prompting questions to spark writing for students, we see that it can also be used as a conversation opener. The images are thought provoking and the questions can form a good anchor for a discussion to build on connections with others.
www.nytimes.com/column/learning-picture-prompt

The **Southern Poverty Law Center** has been offering its resource platform called **Teaching Tolerance** since 1991. They have made their **One World** posters freely available for downloading. These offer an image and sometimes a quote related to equity and inclusion and could be a way to open a conversation in a meeting and frame the discussion for a deeper connection, understand, and level of engagement with each other.
www.tolerance.org/classroom-resources/one-world-posters

I N C L U S I V E

Nurture & embrace differences with empathy instead of polarising

Social Shuffle to Include Others

! **Important note to readers of this *Action Guide for Leaders*:** Even though this Inclusion Nudge is based in a school setting, there are immediate and easy-to-do design applications for workplaces to increase connection, also in online collaboration. So, read on and reflect on how to adapt for your context.

The Challenge

? The in-group and out-group dynamic can have profound implications in society. Outside of the workplace, school, government service offices, public spaces, and civic organisations, it can be hard to expand our interactions with people who are perceived as different from us – the 'others'. To have opportunities where we can form deeper connections with the 'others' can be even rarer. Overall, we tend to be in a bubble of similarity, surrounded by people like ourselves.

Schools have a powerful opportunity to help shift this behaviour early on in children, to widen their learning from experiences with others, and to establish new practices for life. And also, to offer children who are the 'outliers', or deemed less popular, a chance to be included. The challenge is how to break down cliques and popularity groups, to demote exclusion behaviours towards the 'others', and to do this in a way that can have impact and encourage learning more about each other. This is relevant in all social systems and organisations.

This design called the Social Shuffle and research by Prof. Yvonne van den Berg found that students who sit close to each other find them nicer than those who sit further apart. Proximity matters.[50] Here's how she designed a solution to address the change.[51]

Inclusion Nudge Example

The Inclusion Nudge

Use an automated, randomised system to assign where students sit in a classroom, and do every three months so they sit next to new peers.

Purpose: Increase familiarity with other peers by enabling a new seating plan in a classroom, and decrease the tendency to only sit with people you already know and like.

Images from The Social Shuffle website, www.socialshuffle.nl
Over 40 emoji and icons were design by Dawn Amsterdam to be a part of this tool. These are some of them.

77

How To

Fortunately, this is a free online tool to help teachers do this design based on **Yvonne van den Berg's** 🔗 research and supported by **Creative Agency Dawn** 🔗, the health insurer company **Zorg en Zekerheid** 🔗, and **IJsfontein** 🔗. *"This project is a good example of new forms of cooperation; a health insurance company, a university, agencies, developers, producers, schools and teachers."*[52]

A video called "The Social Shuffle case film" is available in English on this tool and can be found on Vimeo. https://vimeo.com/149425150

The Social Shuffle website is currently in Dutch, but with a translator service, you can learn more on their website http://www.socialshuffle.nl/. Here is how they have outlined this process design.

"The Social Shuffle is an easy and free online tool that mixes up the classroom on the basis of a calculation. Four times a year everyone gets a different place. The tool ensures that children are placed in the vicinity of as many different classmates as possible. This way everyone gets to know each other better."

On the ED (European Design) Awards website, they expand further on how they did it:

"We gave it a catchy name – the Social Shuffle – and integrated it in a simple website, optimized for digital school boards, used in almost every Dutch classroom. The Social Shuffle is a shared and fun experience, supported by wacky emojis (see image on previous page), an introductory video and a talking avatar guide. It is designed with classroom environments in mind, where attention spans are short and children are quick to judge on whether something is cool or not. Furthermore, the tool helps shuffling in an optimal way: with every new shuffle, children are sat next to different classmates. And by the end of the year, they all know each other better."[53]

The Social Shuffle has sparked our thinking about how that could happen in a workplace, which is the location where people report that they are most likely to interact with someone who is different from them.[54] There are many benefits to collaboration by sitting with people from all parts of the organisation and learning what they are doing and how your work connects. Also, there are definite 'good' and 'bad' spots of where to sit (next to the manager or for some perhaps away from the manager, or next to the coffee station or for some not there, etc.). Desks could be randomly assigned to all employees in the organisation for a designated period of time (such as quarterly) to give wider exposure and build connections. This can also be a way to encourage innovation, new network building, and collaboration across different teams by even mixing up the seating to be organisation-wide. And make sure that the leaders participate in this as well. Expanding our networks is good for all.

Let us know if you do something similar in your organisation and how has it worked for you. Read on for another design version which can be used when working on distributed teams not sitting together.

Online design version
When people are working from different locations, consider how to apply this design to promote connection with others, especially those who don't know each other at all or as well. Studies show that isolation is often one of the pitfalls of geographically distributed working. Having a sense of being connected with your manager and peers is a strong factor in employee engagement. We see that the Social Shuffle could be adapted to a virtual workplace. Here is how you could do this:

❶ Design
Use an automated program or a simple 'names in a box' to do a randomised assignment of people for a weekly, or even daily, online tea/coffee break with another colleague. This can be for people within a team or from a wider pool across a function or even the entire organisation. Don't forget to have a mix across all roles and levels. If global, be aware of time differences.

Keep it short to naturally replicate the time it would take to drink a beverage with a colleague if they were in the office (10-20 minutes perhaps, really depends on your culture). Have as a default that all are automatically involved in this; they can always opt out for any reason (it is not mandated). Make it easy for people to do this by setting a common time for all across the group for these and send out calendar invites in advance. This shows that social connection is a priority for all and it is as valued as tasks assignments.

When meeting someone new, it can help to have a few prompting questions to get a conversation going. With this intervention, these should be low risk topics but which are open enough to generate sharing in a direction that the person wants to do. Examples of this could be, "What are you drinking?", "What did you have for dinner last night?", "What was your first job?", or have them show and describe an object that is on their desk. Invite all to contribute to the list of discussion questions (co-create). Share these in the calendar invite or in the messaging or display features of your meeting platform, so they are readily available for people to use if they want.

❷ Communicate

Select a title that reflects the culture of your organisation and framed to your mission, values, strategic priorities, and so on. Make it feel that social connection is a part of the approved/supported expectations of working in your organisation's culture. Leaders communicate with the group about the purpose of the initiative – for instance, using a text like below.

"Feeling connected, recognised, and known matters to everyone, and it is important to our success working together. When we work remotely, we don't have the informal chats in the hallway or at the beverage stations. So, let's make this happen in our virtual work by dedicating time to informally connect and get to know our colleagues better and also share about ourselves. This is a time focused on us, not for conducting business meetings or discussing work projects. This is our online coffee/tea break with another colleague. You lead the discussion with each other. It's your time to connect. Join in with your peers and let's get talking!"

❸ Apply

Try it as an experiment over a defined period of time (like 2-4 weeks). Conduct a brief pulse poll with a few of your existing employee engagement survey questions to measure impact pre- & post-program impact. Also, invite open comments from the participants on how the experience was for them.

In-group and out-group formations are here to stay. As human beings, we need this and our tribal mentality is even strengthened in crisis and chaos. But mitigating the negative effects is important for our ability to embrace differences with empathy instead of polarising.

In-group and out-group formations are here to stay. As human beings, we need this and our tribal mentality is even strengthened in crisis and chaos. But mitigating the negative effects is important for our ability to embrace differences with empathy instead of polarising.

Impact

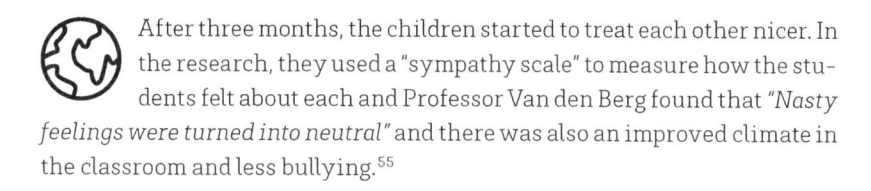

After three months, the children started to treat each other nicer. In the research, they used a "sympathy scale" to measure how the students felt about each and Professor Van den Berg found that *"Nasty feelings were turned into neutral"* and there was also an improved climate in the classroom and less bullying.[55]

"After testing the tool in classrooms with positive results, we started distributing the Social Shuffle to local primary schools, Classrooms in at least 120 schools, we know of, adopted the Social Shuffle, throughout the whole country, contributing to happier classes. Afterwards, the scientists received a prestigious academic award for the societal impact and media attention their research has instigated. But the result that make us the proudest, is that children loved it and that sitting next to an unfamiliar kid has now become something cool."[56]

The Social Shuffle won a Silver award from the ED (European Design) Awards in 2016, plus several other awards.

Authors' Comments & Behavioural Insights

Left up to our system 1 thinking, we often don't fulfil our good intentions towards others who are in our out-group. Professor Binna Kandola highlights one way this can show up in his recent book *Racism at Work*, where he says that in the U.S. *"today, around nine out of ten people respond positively to ...* [the question of 'would you have] *"a Black friend round to dinner?'. However, only 10 % of white people in the USA have Black friends and 68 % have never had a Black person to dinner. Although people agree with the idea of people of different colours mixing socially, they don't do much of it themselves."*[57] This is why this designed intervention of the Social Shuffle can have not only immediate impact at school but also has the potential for shifting who are in our 'friends' circle **(in-group)** later in life. This goes for workplaces and other social settings as well.

Why it works: behavioural insights
This example is an innovative way to have a **randomised** and automated type of checklist to balance out where students or employees sit or work in a classroom or workplace. **Checklists** can take a variety of creative forms as they seek to balance opportunities between in-groups and out-groups. The beauty of this design is that it takes the burden off of the teacher and also off of the students (**reduces the effort** required to do it). The teacher doesn't get 'blamed' for telling who has to sit next to whom, and the students have fun through the use of picture icons and the **gamification** effect.

A study by Professor Ryan D. Enos[58] of Harvard University looked at a commuter train experience as a way to increase exposure to people who are different. In this U.S. study, the views of commuters (83% were White people) on immigration were measured before and over a two-week exposure to other commuters who were Mexican immigrants speaking Spanish (placed by the researchers and something not typical on this train route). In just three days, strong anti-immigration views were expressed by the White people, but after only 10 days these negative views lessened. Professor Enos said, *"these results also suggest that more prolonged contact or interpersonal interaction can diminish initial exclusionary impulse."* This points to the discomfort we may feel by exposure to people who are not in our in-group, but over time they become more familiar and accepted. And this has influence on our views and behaviours. The Mexican immigrants who were recruited to be part of the study reported that at the end of the two weeks, *"People have started to recognize and smile to us."*[59]

Through **positive empathy** toward others, this feeling can become reinforcing, or as researchers at the University of California at Berkeley called it, **"contagious happiness"**.[60] Positive empathy contributes to increased well-being, social connections, and helping behaviour put into action. This helps to further the outcomes from the benefits of connecting with others.

Nurture & embrace differences with empathy instead of polarising

Physical Prompter to Interrupt Bias

The Challenge

Discussions and reviews about talent and performance, as well as decision processes in general, are often biased, despite an intention for meritocracy. The discussions often lack clear design for better quality of objective input. Recent research shows that *"people are more likely to rely on gender, race, and other stereotypes when making* [employee performance] *decisions"*.[61]

One bias is looking for data and facts that confirm existing impressions which leads to increased sharing of rumours, gossip, and judgements instead of real observations. This is the **confirmation bias effect.** That together with the **recency bias,** of only recalling the immediate past rather than the full past year, and the **peak-end bias** of only recalling the peak (positive or negative) and the end, can present an incomplete and inaccurate view of employees' performance. There is a dire need of a redesign. Here is a simple process design that anyone can implement in their next performance appraisal review meeting to help de-bias the process.

The Inclusion Nudge

Have a physical prompter on the meeting table for all in the group to use whenever they believe that bias is pushing into the discussion.

Purpose: Call to attention when bias arises in discussions to help mitigate the biased effect, and thereby, increase objectivity and shift the mode of thinking of the evaluators or participants from that of stereotype associative to reflective. The purpose is also to enable behavioural change in the moment.

How To

Use prompters, such as visual, auditory, and physical cues. Here are several variations on this design that you can do based on your own context.

Version 1: Reception Bell

Axel Jentzsch, a former European inclusion and diversity leader at BASF, implemented in meetings the use of a reception bell as a physical prompter to interrupt bias during talent evaluation discussions. All managers were given a hotel reception bell to put on the meeting table in front of them. They were instructed to make immediate use of this bell whenever they experienced or suspected that someone was sharing an assumption, bias, stereotype, rumour, or gossip rather than a real personal experience or facts about performance, or whenever the experience was presented not as a neutral observation but as a judgement.

Wherever bias can be interrupted, there is a need for simple ways to do this. And it's important to empower everybody to do it. The reception bell is a playful disruption. There are many other ways on how this could be done; here are some that we've used in our work with organisations around the world.

Version 2: Knock, knock

Don't have a hotel bell? Then, use another auditory cue for when bias may be occurring in the discussion, such as knocking on the table. **Lisa Kepinski,** Founder of Inclusion Institute, has worked with teams in Switzerland and Germany, where knocking on the table is sometimes used in lieu of hand clapping applause. Perhaps in these teams, this made the knocking action feel more familiar and comfortable to do, rather than in other cultures that may not be using this nonverbal form of communicating. The key is to make it easy to do **(simplicity)**. Consider what could work within your organisation and culture to call attention to potential bias in a discussion.

Version 3: Bias sign
Lisa Kepinski worked with a team where they decided to use a sign with the word 'BIAS' on it. This worked for them. They had all agreed that this was the mechanism that they'd like to use to call out bias. It was simple (straight to the point) and easy (no cost, no fancy equipment needed) to make the sign. This could be done in any meeting with just a piece of paper and a pen. So, they could implement it anytime and anywhere. It was not dependent upon remembering to bring a bell. However, this approach is one that needs caution as well. For most groups, Lisa wouldn't want to use this without advance discussions on the context. One of the downsides of this approach could be that the person being called out can feel targeted, shamed, and blamed by having the 'BIAS' sign flashed at them. A high level of respect, trust, openness to receiving feedback, and commitment by all to objectivity are needed for this to work well. A team culture that is flatter rather than hierarchical is also important for success, as **status risk** may lead to **self-silencing** and not calling out bias in those with higher status. Also, process check-ins are needed to ensure this approach is working towards the intention of calling out bias rather than slipping into negative outcomes (sustaining bias rather than mitigating it).

Version 4: Interrupt the interrupter
Phrases can be used to help steer conversations veering towards biased behaviours. **Tinna** and **Lisa** recommend to use this technique to stop interruption patterns in team discussions. Research shows that women are interrupted nearly 3 times more often than men, and this interruption is done by *both* women and men to women. It's a socialised norm that its 'ok' to interrupt women more than men. To shift this pattern, we've worked with teams to apply this Inclusion Nudge to call out when interruptions happen to anyone on the team. We call this the 'Interrupt the Interrupter' and it works much like the hotel bell or red card interventions. The intent is not to blame or shame the interrupter, but to call out the behaviour. This allows the speaking to revert back to the original speaker rather than to the interrupter.

Try using phrases like:

"I'd like to hear what .... has to say! He was interrupted"
".......... is still speaking and it's important for us to hear those thoughts now"
"Let her speak, please."

These help to shift back to the speaker. You may want to use a checklist to track how often interruption is occurring and the trends over time by using this intervention. Review this as a group.

Impact

This *Process Design* Inclusion Nudge helps people understand how often and how quickly bias, subjective judgement, and interruptions sneak into discussions, conversations, and decision-making processes. In talent development discussions, these interventions are useful when evaluations deviate from the objective exchange of facts and observations and allowed managers to quickly get back on track.

Authors' Comments & Behavioural Insights

The cost of a biased review process is high with loss of talent potential, engagement, and retention. Using a flawed process perpetuates poor management practices and overconfidence in the talent evaluation outcomes. Biases can have hugely negative impact on people in the **out-group** or minority staff members by not receiving the same opportunities for career development, advancement, and compensation as those who are in the **in-group** or those who fit the cultural norms. This happens under the guise of a talent process that is seemingly based on meritocracy. Yet, the more merit based an organisation feels that it is, the higher rates of discrimination due to false comfort and certainty that biases don't occur.[62]

Why it works: behavioural insights
Biases can impair objectivity of talent and performance discussions and decision-making processes. We all can fall prey to these. Some of these are listed below.

Confirmation bias is when we selectively recall and see only what fits with our original impression, and thus strengthen our biased view.

Halo & horns bias is when an irrelevant context or associative reference can influence seeing the actual performance, such as with the halo effect if the employee is on a team lead by a manager who is favoured by the head of the organisation and by extension a more positive assessment of the employee carries over merely by association with the star manager. Or with the horns effect, if an employee reminds the manager of someone else that she/he didn't like in the past, then a cloud of negative association taints the objectivity.

Recency bias is when we only clearly recall the past few weeks performance and not the full year performance.

Stereotypes and implicit associations, such as women are seen as more naturally collaborative and thus not rated as highly on this competency as men. Or men are seen as lower performing when they have a strength on team work or are perceived as too soft, and hence perceived as not fitting male leadership norms. There is repeated research showing that women receive a penalty in ratings on leadership competencies and women receive more vague criticism and shorter reviews than men. Studies show that the feedback given to women has to do with their personalities and tone, as compared to men to who received constructive feedback focused on their technical skills. And there are extra layers of evaluation applied to employees who are not mirroring the majority.[63]

These, and many other biases, work against our best intentions for fair appraisals of performance and good decision-making. By designing a way to call out when these may be happening, we can interrupt their impact on the process. And by doing this as a collective evaluating team, more people are focused on working together to achieve better outcomes, which strengthens the performance evaluation process. This team-based approach lessens the burden of having just one person call out bias. De-biasing becomes a group norm. As does making sure that we all contribute to nurturing and embracing differences.

INCLUSIVE

WHAT & HOW
I'll make sure to nurture & embrace differences with empathy instead of polarising

INCLUSIVE

Conquer outdated social norms & discriminatory practices instead of maintaining them

'Flexible Work' as the Default in the Job Request Form

The Challenge

Often the ability to work flexibly (time, structure, location) is limited to just a few people in an organisation making flexible working an exception, even when many may wish to work in this way. For example, across all generations of the workforce, surveys show that each age group expresses a desire for more control over their ways of getting work done. For organisations, this can be a critical factor in talent attraction and retention. Done well, it can boost productivity and engagement. However, one of the common challenges is ensuring more flexible work arrangements are available for all employees, and not just positioned as for some, such as working mothers or tech workers.

The Inclusion Nudge

Make all roles 'flexible'

Set a pre-selected default for all jobs to be 'flexible working' in the online form for job requests used by hiring managers in the organisation's recruitment process

Purpose: Ensure equity for all employees across all in the organisation by making flexible working the norm, rather than the exception. Setting the default to be flexible working is an effective way to make inclusion the default in the system, culture, and behaviour.

How To

This is a simple redesign of an existing process if your organisation is already using online forms for submitting job requests. If not, this can easily be integrated in other forms or processes. You might even want to create one.

1. Automatically have as organisational-wide standard text for all job descriptions 'Flexible working is our norm'.

2. Design the online form for submitting a job request by hiring managers to have 'flexible working' as the pre-selected default for the job format.

→ You should carefully consider how you frame up alternative options for job formats other than 'flexible working', such as 'working in the office full-time'.

→ We recommend that you add a 'If not, why not' reasoning by instructing the hiring managers, if they want to opt out of the 'flexible working' job format, to document logical constraints about time and place. If they want to opt out and not support flexible working, at least that has to be a deliberate choice and not an unconscious action. The approach changes the thinking from "Can this job be done through other ways of working, such as flexibly and / or in another location?" to "Why would this job not be suitable for flexible ways of working?". That is an important difference in reasoning.

You can also use the Inclusion Nudge **'IF NOT, WHY NOT' ACCOUNTABILITY** (→ page 166) to support this change.

3. If a hiring manager choses another job format option than 'flexible working', initiate a discussion about potential solutions around 'logical constraints'

We recommend that you engage the employees in such job functions or similar jobs in co-creating solutions for a job design that makes flexible working possible to some extent. They often have important insights to do this.

4. Advertise all jobs at all levels with 'flexible working' explicitly communicated as the norm in the organisation.

Here are some other actions you can do to supplement this default design, which have been implemented in organisations that **Tinna C. Nielsen,** Founder of Move the Elephant for Inclusiveness, and **Lisa Kepinski,** Founder of Inclusion Institute, have worked with.

A checklist

To support working in different locations (some call this 'remote work' or 'virtual working'), design a checklist with information about what kinds of support and technology people need to do some or all of their activities in a flexible manner (for example from a home office or a work hub). Don't leave this to chance. The checklist helps to ensure that managers can equally provide the same support to each employee. This reduces complexity, and thus, increases the likelihood that managers will make the changes needed for each employee to perform their best.

We recommend this checklist to be designed in a collaboration with employees, hiring manager, and human resources.

Do an audit and show the gap

Use an evidenced-based approach by doing an audit of how many of your organisation's job descriptions actually have flexible work mentioned. In one organisation we worked with, the senior leaders believed their supportive comments for flex work would have impact, but a review of all job postings over six months showed less than 15 % actually had the words 'flexible working'. This data was shared with the senior leaders who were shocked about the gap between talking about their intentions and this actually being done as a standard practice. The 'aha' realisation from seeing the data triggered greater leadership support for the process design to make this the default in all job postings. Due to the gap between intentions and actions, it's important to design the job request submission form to have 'flexible working' as the default. This way you make it easy for managers to opt-in on flexible working because that is already the system default.

Call it 'agile' instead of 'flexible'

Reframe the perceptions by using the word 'agile' instead of 'flexible'. This is a way to change the **anchor** of the thought process from a past-held perception of flexible work arrangements being a 'women's issue' to now being an organisational productivity issue with connotations to future proofing the organisation through agility. Also, reframe terms like 'virtual work' or 'remote work' (working in a location not physically with your team) to remove any negative designation of 'virtual' as not 'real' work and 'remote' as not with us or outliers. Replace these terms with 'new ways of working' or simply; 'it's just how we work here' (it's the **default**), or just call it 'work'.

Impact

One example of an organisation using the online job request form with 'flexible working' set as the default option, is the telecommunication company Telstra headquartered in Australia. They have succeeded in making flexible working the default and norm with their 'All Roles Flex' programme. This began in 2013 with a pilot which was successful and with the CEO as the sponsor, it expanded company-wide in 2014. They saw an increase in diversity of applicants to the company and an increase in employee engagement. Their 'All Roles Flex' approach is covered on their website under the Careers section, and there are several articles written about their experience[64]

Making 'flexible working' the norm in an organisation, increases well-being, stress reduction, retention, and engagement of staff. It can also make it easier to attract international candidates who might not be internationally mobile for relocation but are available for commuting. Additional impacts could be the potential for lower real estate needs due to less people in the office, and for society, there is less pollution from commuters every day.

Authors' Comments & Behavioural Insights

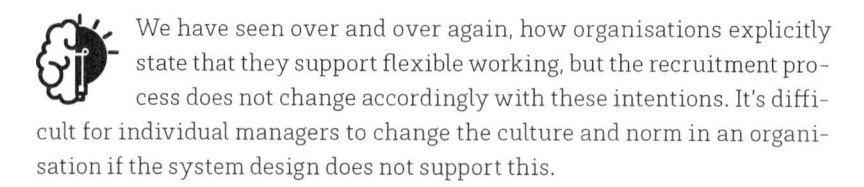

We have seen over and over again, how organisations explicitly state that they support flexible working, but the recruitment process does not change accordingly with these intentions. It's difficult for individual managers to change the culture and norm in an organisation if the system design does not support this.

Conquer outdated social norms & discriminatory practices
instead of maintaining them

Interrupt Gender Caregiver Stereotype with Images

The Challenge

Unconscious thinking plays a big part in maintaining outdated social norms and, at times, discriminatory practices. It can interfere with realising inclusion of all by reinforcing stereotypes and outdated ways of interacting through images, designs, and symbols. These can also indicate and continue unspoken cultural norms, such as *"Who is a leader?"*, *"Who are the 'heroes'?"*, *"Who are caretakers?"* The images limit our thinking and block realising the full value of diversity. Because these images are seemingly permanent and part of the building or the environment around us, these often go unnoticed or unchallenged when trying to increase inclusion in the organisation. What we see is what we believe.

Tests and research show that the majority of people implicitly associate certain traits with people based on unconsciously-held stereotypical mental models. One of these is that of *"caregivers are women"*, regardless of what we know about men actually being caregivers. This inaccurate mental perception harms both women and men, and results in many limitations on opportunities and realising full potential. By changing the implicit associations by presenting more accurate depictions of caregiving will have a crucial impact on unconscious perceptions of women and men both as caregivers; and a more equal supporting structure enabling both to fulfil caregiving in their personal and work lives.

As leaders, we need to pay attention to the images and stereotypes surrounding us and the people we lead, and take action to diversify these when needed.

The Inclusion Nudge

Change the implicit association of women = caregivers by also framing caregiving with the male gender.

See these images below as examples of how to do this.

Purpose: Prime a specific association in the unconscious of 'man = caregiver' by using images to interrupt unconscious mental associations and more accurately depict reality and the desired potential opportunities and outcomes.

The above three pictures in Helsinki and in Tokyo taken by Ursula A. Wynhoven in 2014 & 2019.

Left and middle: *Photos taken by Lisa Kepinski in Copenhagen in 2014. Signs outside men's and women's toilets in a workplace.*

Right: *Photo taken by Stephen Frost in 2019 inside an airplane.*

95

How To

❶ Identify images portraying stereotypes of various roles or functions, such as leaders, engineers, politicians, coders, doctors, nurses, and others. Identify the patterns.

❷ Display images of people in a wide variety of roles to counter the impact of implicit associations, like the examples above that were submitted by **Ursula A. Wynhoven**, a United Nations representative to the ITC, **Stephen Frost**, CEO of Frost Included, and **Lisa Kepinski,** Founder of Inclusion Institute.

❸ Strategically put these in important and frequently-used places in your organisation, community, school, or city, including in postings of open positions, meeting rooms, and internal communication, or depict images on the sidewalk in cities, as they do in Helsinki.

How you get buy-in for making the change

If you find it difficult to get buy-in for making changes in images, signs, pictures, and office design, then you can design a *Feel the Need* Inclusion Nudge to help people to see the purpose for this change. You can take pictures of the images, communication, signs, messages, interior, and engage them in spotting the patterns and stereotypes. Or you can even engage your colleagues in taking the photos to give them ownership and to influence the ways they view the environment around them.

One of the ways to do this is the **"Inclusion Hunt". Lisa Kepinski** designed this and has used it in several organisations that she worked with as a way to engage all people in conducting an audit of the images, designs, and symbols that can be reinforcing stereotypes within their workplace. This includes women as caregivers, and also other stereotypes. All people are requested to *"bring their critical thinking and seeing"* (this is an example of **priming**) to spot where exclusion may be happening in the language, images, and designs in the workplace or community. This participatory data-gathering experience can easily be done by anyone.

These are examples of what have been spotted.

- no gender-neutral toilets in any offices worldwide
- all conference rooms named after Western men
- all women's toilets being also the 'disabled' toilet (no men's toilets were 'disabled')
- the only wheelchair-accessible entrance to the headquarters building was not at the front and entering the lobby, but down a side alley and through a rear entrance
- majority of images and stories about flexible working showcasing the benefits for only working mothers (no mention of other life reasons and very few examples working fathers)
- Staff communications in the headquarters of a global organisation were only in the local language and the international staff could not understand them

This type of participatory audit can be an essential first step to change the images, symbols, names, designs, etc. to be more inclusive of all and to mirror the desired intentions for inclusion. *What would your staff uncover in an Inclusion Hunt in your organisation? Why not ask them?* Engage *'the people it's about'.*

Authors' Comments & Behavioural Insights

In the field of advertising, many countries have placed legal bans or adopted guidelines to counter perpetuating gender, racial, and other froms of stereotypes in public marketing campaigns. These are harmful and not representative of real life, for example by showing only women as responsible for housekeeping or men as inept at childcare. The UK Advertising Standards Authority rolled out such a ban in 2019.[65] Other countries with similar bans include Belgium, France, Norway, South Africa, and India.[66] This momentum is expected to continue in more countries. *How do you communicate with people inside and outside of your organisation? How does this shape their perception of your organisation or community?*

Why it works: behavioural insights

Professor Iris Bohnet writes in her book *What Works* about changes made at Harvard University's Kennedy School of Government with the portraits of alumni and other artistic scenes on the school's walls to be more representative across gender and race/ethnicity. Students brought attention to this **imbalance of images**. She describes that in March 2012, of the 60+ people who were depicted in the art work were all men, except for 3 women who were all shown in traditional **female caregiving roles**. *What does the art in your organisation reflect about the cultural norms, behaviours, and views of talent?*

Additionally, think of when people enter your workplace or visit your website and see the portraits of the past and current leaders. How diverse are these? Some organisations remove these images to hide their poor representation across diversity. While for others, they may use the images to signal something they want to convey about their culture. These organisations post photos of all leaders and partners or employees as a large group photo. This image shift shows a **flip in perception** from focusing on just a few at the top to an employee-centric organisation with values on the employee experience rather than on a hierarchy. *What do your images convey to visitors, employees, and leaders about your culture?*

The use of **counterculture images** and **role models** has been used in attracting more men to the nursing profession. Compassionate caregiving is a human capacity, not limited to only women. Furthermore, patients benefit by having diversity in the care staff.[67] Many countries have a nursing shortage, and at the same time are facing unemployment due to shifting labour markets (such as a loss of manufacturing jobs). As a way to address this, efforts have turned to encouraging men to become nurses. In the U.S., there has been an increase of men in nursing roles from 2.2% in 1960 to 13% in 2017, and a comprehensive research study has shown that *"liberalizing gender role attitudes explains around 50 percent of the growth"*.[68] Images to shift the perception of who is a nurse have helped. In the U.S., the Oregon Center for Nursing has posters targeting men and asking *"Are you man enough to be a nurse?"*.[69] While in Scotland, *"less than 10% of nursing students are male, a figure that has hardly changed in the past 10 years."* To help shift perceptions *"by showcasing positive male nursing role models ... the University of Dundee launched its '#MenDoCare' campaign, aimed at increasing the number of male applicants"*[70] to its nursing program in 2018. *"Recent figures from the Uni-*

versities and Colleges Admissions Service show male applicants for nursing courses in Scotland were up."[71] Other efforts have looked at the placement of the counterculture images, such as the University of Texas which wanted to increase the number of male nurses and placed its advertisements for nurses on the sports page of the newspaper.[72]

Framing is one of the key aspects in **choice architecture** and nudging. How something is positioned or portrayed (framed) can reflect and shape mindsets. By taking a fresh look at your organisation, it helps to surface symbols, images, tokens of perhaps a previous perspective that may not be currently true or in alignment with your organisation's commitment to inclusion, equity, belonging, and diversity. Often, we don't question our physical environment, seemingly accepting it as *'the way it is'*. Yet, framing impacts our unconscious thinking and can have far more power than words. If we are driving culture change, then this needs to extend to our physical workplaces and communities, as well. This *Framing Perceptions* Inclusion Nudge helps to ensure stereotypes are not supported by images in the workplace and society. Seeing your usual surroundings in a new perspective is called **'perspective taking'** and is a powerful influencer on perceptions and behaviour.

INCLUSIVE

Conquer outdated social norms & discriminatory practices instead of maintaining them

Experience Disability in Real Meetings

The Challenge

To create awareness, change discriminatory practices, and build abilities to collaborate and lead inclusively, it will make a difference to experience how it feels to not be part of the majority. Throughout the course of normal business, a team in an organisation explored what it may be like to experience a physical disability and how it changes communicating with their peers. Here is how they did this.

The Inclusion Nudge

Simulate an experience of a physical disability while conducting normal business, such as in the dark or blindfolded (to prevent seeing), silenced (to prevent verbal engagement), arms tied (to prevent expressing themselves with body language or in writing), ear plugs (to mimic hearing loss), and/or individuals confined to wheelchairs.

Purpose: Get a small glimpse into what it would be like to communicate and participate in meetings for people with a physical disability to motivate for more inclusive behaviours.

How To

❗ If you adapt this design to your organisation, be sure to engage people with different abilities to understand their real experiences in meetings in your workplace or community. One way to do this is to make an open invitation to all people in the organisation to contribute with suggestions. We should not assume who has a disability or who doesn't, as 7 out 10 of us will have some form of a disability in our lifetimes and often these are hidden. Another way to do this is to engage with a people with disabilities network or with a local NGO / community services organisation for people with disabilities. Reach out to them and co-design the version of this Inclusion Nudge in your context. It's important to work with 'the people it's about'. This will ensure relevancy, accuracy, and lead to better solutions be developed.

❶ Prepare
Before the meeting starts, participants are assigned a physical disability, relevant to their normal working style if applicable. For example, extroverts were silenced, individuals with expressive tendencies were prevented from using their arms to complement their talking, etc. Normal business was conducted without means purposefully established to enable those with disabilities.

❷ During meeting
Facilitate the meeting as you would normally do. Post-meeting, the team spends 15 minutes debriefing on the experience by asking questions such as

What key learnings were experienced?
How did the disability effect your personal engagement and effectiveness of contribution during the meeting?
How did our team positively enable those with difference?
How will you lead differently after this experience?

❸ Follow up
Consider doing the experience again later (if possible), but this time apply the Inclusion Nudges **WRITE BEFORE TALKING TO REDUCE GROUP DYNAMICS** (→ page 55) or **SHARE WITH A PEER TO ACCESS DIVERSITY IN GROUPS** (→ page 109) and debrief with the group how this made a difference – if and if not, why and why not. Discuss other ways to have meetings that would be more inclusive.

Impact

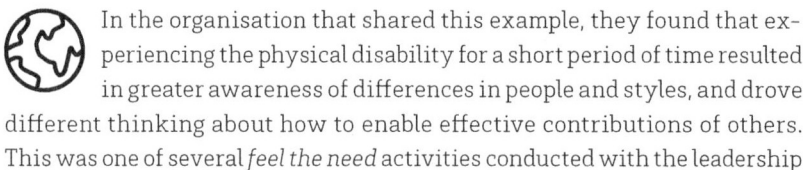

In the organisation that shared this example, they found that experiencing the physical disability for a short period of time resulted in greater awareness of differences in people and styles, and drove different thinking about how to enable effective contributions of others. This was one of several *feel the need* activities conducted with the leadership team to increase awareness of the impact of privilege from multiple angles.

Authors' Comments & Behavioural Insights

This experience can be so powerful, and we highly recommend that you consider doing the experience again later to harvest learnings from the experience and to engage the participants in finding more inclusive solutions. Only this time apply the Inclusion Nudges **WRITE BEFORE TALKING TO REDUCE GROUP DYNAMICS** (→ page 55) or **SHARE WITH A PEER TO ACCESS DIVERSITY IN GROUPS** (→ page 109) and debrief with the group how this made a difference – if and if not, why and why not. Discuss other ways to have meetings that would be more inclusive. Then test these moving forward.

Why it works: behavioural insights

Experiencing limitations that others experience is an impactful way to engage people in challenging unreflected social norms and discriminatory practices instead of maintaining them unintentionally. Research shows how experiencing and sometimes merely hearing about other people being treated badly, discriminated, and socially excluded triggers the area of the brain where physical pain and **empathy** is located, even when we're not directly experiencing it ourselves. Feeling the experiences of colleagues motivates us to want to change this.[73]

This example is from a workplace, but this is equally important to use when engaging with politicians, civil servants, city developers, architects, teachers, citizens, and communities. Too often people who do not have a disability (physical or mental) need to feel it to change their perspectives and to be inclusive.

INCLUSIVE

> **WHAT & HOW**
> I'll make sure to conquer outdated social norms & discriminatory practices instead of maintaining them

INCLUSIVE

Leverage diversity of perspectives & backgrounds instead of under-utilising people's abilities & the mix

Start with 'Critical Thinking' Statement

The Challenge

Social norms play a role in all groups and these influence members in a group to conform or to silence themselves. This is a strong group dynamic because people fear social sanctioning, punishment, and have concern for their reputation. This means that they don't disclose and share information or opinions that depart from the group's inclination. In groups that are inclusive and welcome deviating views and/or competing information, then the social norms foster a different type of behaviour. This should not be left up to chance, but should be the default of any type of group interactions. This is how easily it can be done.

The Inclusion Nudge

As an integrated part of facilitating meetings and collaborating say out loud and/or write so it's visible to the group members:

'The task at hand requires critical thinking.'

Purpose: Prime group members with this statement to perceive that their task and goal is to arrive at the right solution, and thus, they are more likely to disclose what they know and think.

How To

This *Process Design* Inclusion Nudge is so simple. When you facilitate a meeting or collaborate in a group or team, do these steps.

→ Literally say out loud *"This task requires critical thinking"*.

→ Do this in both with in-person meetings and online meetings.

→ Also, write the statement on the walls or whiteboard in the room, or on the virtual meeting platform's whiteboard to make sure it's visible, present, and salient at all times during meeting. In online meetings, you can make it pop up from time to time as a reminder.

Impact

When a group is primed with 'critical thinking' they engage more in **constructive confrontations** and they are far more likely to disclose what they know.[74] In a healthy team culture, team members think critically and they do not always get along, and due to this they perform better.[75] Also, in groups where the members are not united by close social ties, they benefit more from dissent and diversity.[76] The aim should not be for everyone to 'get along'. Saying that a task requires 'getting along' has been identified in research to trigger a perception that the task is to be friendly with each other, and thus, they challenge each other's perspectives and viewpoints less and self-silence more.

Authors' Comments & Behavioural Insights

An inclusive leader and team will make sure they prime critical thinking at all times in any kind of collaboration they engage in.

Why it works: behavioural insights

Priming is important because basically everything around us, such as a word on a wall, a title of a game, requested information about our gender before a test, and more, prompt our behaviours and perspectives in a specific direction. Priming is like 'cues' that **trigger specific associa-**

tions and perceptions in the unconscious mind and affect people's choices and behaviour.

For these reasons, priming should not be left up to chance, but be a deliberate choice to use systematically and consciously as an integrated part of collaboration and decision making, as well as a means to change social norms to be more inclusive of diverse perspectives and identities.

Many studies have proven the priming effect of words. This experiment shows how we are influenced by things that we don't even realise. Students (18-22 years old) were instructed to assemble four-word sentences from a set of five words. The group that had words associated with elderly, such as forgetful, bald, gray, or wrinkle, walked significantly slower when asked to walk to another room after the experiment than the group of student who had random (neutral) words. This was due to two kinds of priming. The set of words primed thoughts of old age, without mentioning the word 'old' and these thoughts primed a behaviour of walking slowly, which is associated with old age. All the students insisted that nothing they did after doing the scrambled sentences could have been influenced by the words they had worked with.[77]

And this effect is also present in collaboration and problem solving. As bizarre as this might sound, it more bizarre to believe this does not influence you, so let's make sure to use this mental mechanism of priming for something good.

Leverage diversity of perspectives & backgrounds instead of under-utilising people's abilities & the mix

Invite a 'Skills Pitch' from Everyone

The Challenge

Often when selecting employees, residents, or citizens to be part of solving a problem or being part of a project team, it is a biased process. The same people are often appointed or invited again and again based on the leader's knowledge about their skills and competence or simply based on the leader's assumptions. Studies show that managers often don't know enough about their employees' skills, and the number 1 reason that people leave their job is because their skills are under-utilised. Research finds that 62% of employees would like their skills to be used and valued better.[78]

Biased processes not only leave a lot of potential and talent under-utilised, but additionally lead to the same kind of solutions being reproduced. This also results in inequality in opportunities to contribute and grow, and as a consequence leading to disengagement, missed opportunities, and the feeling of disempowerment.

The Inclusion Nudge

Invite everyone in a team or a community to write a pitch on how their skills and knowledge can contribute to solving the task at hand, including a short motivational statement for why they should be part of the project group.

Purpose: Give people and yourself a new opportunity to redefine their role and change stuck patterns of what kind of tasks they are assigned and invited to solve. Get access to the diversity in a group of people.

How To

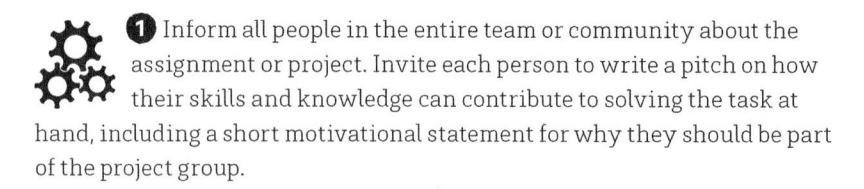

① Inform all people in the entire team or community about the assignment or project. Invite each person to write a pitch on how their skills and knowledge can contribute to solving the task at hand, including a short motivational statement for why they should be part of the project group.

② Instruct them to write it anonymously, so they are not identifiable. Find a way to keep this anonymity intact throughout the process of evaluation and selection to mitigate bias. Have a neutral person coordinate the process to avoid bias influencing the selection process and ensure focus on the skills needed and not on the person.

③ Make sure to use a structured process where you map out the skills people find relevant for solving the task. This will help you compose a team of people that cover these skills and competences.

④ When you have selected the people, ask the coordinator to reveal the identity, so you can reach out to them and let them know they have been chosen. Make sure to let the others know that they were not selected and that their skills pitch was a valuable contribution to define how to move forward with the project. Also, let them know if you now have new insights about their skills and competences.

⑤ Make sure you follow up on this in later conversations, employee appraisal, and other feedback sessions. Make a plan with each person, how to better make use of their skills and talents.

The Impact

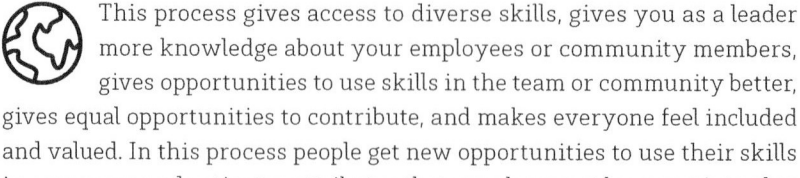

This process gives access to diverse skills, gives you as a leader more knowledge about your employees or community members, gives opportunities to use skills in the team or community better, gives equal opportunities to contribute, and makes everyone feel included and valued. In this process people get new opportunities to use their skills in new ways and activates attributes that may have not been put into play in their current role and the assignments that they have previously been engaged.

INCLUSIVE

Leverage diversity of perspectives & backgrounds
instead of under-utilising people's abilities & the mix

Share with a Peer to Access Diversity in Groups

The Challenge

Even when the intentions to be inclusive in group work are present, it can be difficult to do in practice. This is due to invisible and unintentional group dynamics and biases, formal and informal power, status and roles in a group, self-silencing, and much more. Speaking up in plenary can be a vulnerable situation for many people and especially when having a point of view that differs from that of the majority. In this unstructured approach of *'just speak up'*, the input offered may favour the most fluent, people with communication styles that match the cultural norms, those with more power and status, members of the majority, etc. These factors can result in less input and making it easier to remain silent and go along with a view already expressed. All of this limits access to the diversity of perspectives that is so crucial in task solving, innovation, and decision making. Rather than leaving this to chance and good wishes, we need to design the facilitation process to ensure psychological safety, and to be inclusive by default.

The Inclusion Nudge

Each member in the group shares their perspective with one other person (peer) in the group.

They, then, share each other's perspectives to the larger group in plenary.

Purpose: Ensure all people feel safe to share their perspective (this intervention does require a level of trust in the group), ensure that individuals do not conform to the view of majority of group members, and ensure that communication misunderstandings are captured and corrected.

How To:

❶ The facilitator shares a challenge, task, or problem that needs to be discussed, changed, or solved.

❷ Each member in the group shares their perspective with one other person (peer) in the group – preferably those standing next to each other

❸ They share each other's perspectives to the larger group in plenary.

❹ We also recommend you to consider a silent sense check of a decision. Having made a decision, ask all participants to share with their colleague, what they understand was just been decided. As a pair, they share with the larger group. Often, the decision turns out to be understood in many different ways. Always allow extra time for further discussion and to reconvene. Make sure everyone is aligned and has understood the same thing.

Online design version
Make sure you do this in online meetings as well.

→ Before the meeting, participants team up in pairs.
→ Let them know who they have been teamed up with. Send them each others' name and contact information.
→ Make breaks during the meeting for the 'peers' to call each other and share.
→ Invite them to share each others' view verbally or by writing in the chat.

Impact

Tinna C. Nielsen, Founder of Move the Elephant for Inclusiveness, and **Lisa Kepinski,** Founder of Inclusion Institute, have shared this simple intervention with thousands of leaders and teams around the world, and the feedback is very positive. The majority of leaders apply this way of facilitating on a regular basis. They report higher inclusivity engagement in their teams.

This intervention turned out, in the manufacturing company where Tinna previously worked, to be ideal to use in business planning sessions, team development sessions, LEAN processes (LEAN Board meetings), and leadership team meetings. It was appreciated by many workers because for those who did not feel comfortable writing, then speaking with a peer, enabled them to share more.

By implementing ways of working that automatically leverage diversity of thought, you do not rely only on awareness, reflection, extroverts, or those that 'speak up'. The majority of people having gone through this process, apply this Inclusion Nudge and involve their teams in doing the same.

Authors' Comments & Behavioural Insights

This intervention is an impactful way to make inclusion in groups the default and norm without having to talk about inclusivity. It just makes it an automatic and integrated part of the process design. It's such a simple way to make sure people feel heard and listened to, that the diversity of the perspectives, backgrounds, and abilities are utilised and leveraged.

Why it works: behavioural insights

You can get many other examples of how to do this in the World Economic Forum article that Tinna and Lisa wrote entitled *"11 Ways to Outsmart Your Brain and Be a Better Leader"*[79] as well as in *The Inclusion Nudges Guidebook* and the other books in this Action Guide Series.

INCLUSIVE

> **WHAT & HOW**
> I'll make sure to leverage diversity of perspectives & backgrounds instead of under-utilising people's abilities & the mix

INCLUSIVE

Undermine the negative impact of unconscious biases instead of focusing on awareness

Ask Flip Questions to Change Your Perceptions in the Moment

The Challenge

It can be difficult to see how biases affect us and it's almost impossible to be consciously aware of our unconscious reactions in the moment as we are interacting with other people. As individuals we hold many unconscious biases about other people. Since these are often hidden to us and also sometimes work against our own intentions and self-perception as fair, bias plays out in micro-behaviours that result in a waste of human resources and inequality. The challenge is how to avoid that our biases negatively influence the way we perceive, judge, evaluate, listen, talk, and behave. How can we challenge our biases in our interactions with other people when we can't control them and it is too difficult to be aware of all our biases? And more importantly, how do we change our perceptions and behaviour in the moment, in the situation?

Tinna C. Nielsen, Founder of Move the Elephant for Inclusiveness, and **Lisa Kepinski,** Founder of Inclusion Institute, have used what we call "Flip Questions" for over a decade to address this and we still do. Our biases do not disappear just because we know a lot about bias. Here is how we do it.

The Inclusion Nudge

Ask Flip Questions silently to yourself – in your head as you are in the moment – as you are interacting with people.

Here are a few examples:

"If she was a man, would I have responded differently to what he just did?"

or

"If he was not 25 years old, but had 25 years more experience than me, would I have listened differently to what he just said?"

Purpose: Flip and counter your immediate perception (bias, stereotypes, preconception) in the moment of interaction. It's about creating a trigger in our body to realise our own biased thinking. This can help us change our unconscious thought processes and change our behaviours in the moment.

How To

You ask the questions silently to yourself – in your head, but you can also ask them out loud to other people and groups of people to help them reflect and see from another perspective. Ask yourself Flip Question as you are interacting with people, such as listening to them talk or share an idea or give a presentation or other situations. Where there are people, there are biases, so Flip Questions are relevant to apply everywhere.

How to design Flip Questions
You start the question with *"If ..."* and then you frame a question based on some of the visible characteristics of the other person or some insights you have about your own biases or some insights from surveys or other sources about specific biases or stereotypes. When framing the question, the aim is to find the opposite perspective.

Let's use height as an example of how bias can influence us in many ways, and how you can frame a variety of Flip Questions to counter this. If you know you have a positive bias towards tall people (perhaps because you are tall yourself or because you are influenced by the stereotype that tall people are an authority) then counter that bias by asking yourself Flip Questions such as these below.

"If he/she was NOT tall like me, would I then ask more critical questions?" or

"If he was not so short, would I think he was more competent?" or

"If she/he was not the tallest candidate, would I ask different kinds of questions right now?"

If you know the data (from research)[80] about the tallest candidates being selected for leadership positions, then most people want to make sure that kind of bias does not influence their evaluation of the candidate's merit and their decision about who to hire for a leadership position.* To counter this, you can ask yourself Flip Questions, such as the suggested examples above, and you can also supplement Flip Questions with a couple of questions to highlight the absurdity of bias. Adding a bit of playfulness to the seriousness of the situation has also proven to be effective in changing our perception. Here are a couple of examples below.

"Are tall people better leaders because they are tall?" or

"Are tall people better at executing on strategy because they have long legs and are taller than the others?"

> *To learn more about this height bias, see the **ACTION GUIDE FOR TALENT SELECTION** with 30 Inclusion Nudges to mitigate bias.

Inspiration to design your Flip Questions

There are no limitations for what kind of Flip Questions you can ask. Remember to also ask Flip Questions to other people and groups you work with. We have listed a bunch of examples of Flip Questions we have used to counter our own biases. We hope you find inspiration in these to make your own.

- *If she was a man and not a woman,*
  would I interpret her as frustrated instead of hysterical as I just did?

- *If he was slim and not overweight,*
  would I perceive what he just said as more credible?

- *If she was smiling more, would I find her more likable?*

- *If he was less aggressive, would I ask more critical questions?*

- *If the pitch of his voice was deeper and not so high,*
  would I listen more to the content of what he is saying?

- *If she did not have a disability, would I speak so slowly and loud to her?*

- *If he did not have a dark skin colour, would I feel less sceptical?*

- *If he had not been positioned as an expert by the CEO,*
  would I then speak up with my knowledge about the flaws in his data?

- *If she was less introvert in her communication style,*
  would I listen more interested and passionate?

- *If she was less extrovert and loud in her presentation style,*
  would I listen more to the content of her presentation?

- *If she was a man, what salary would I offer him?*

- *If he wore a suit, would I have seen him as a better leader?*

- *If this candidate did not graduate from the same school as me,*
  would I have said they were as well-prepared?

- *If his tattoo was not visible, would I have felt safer around him?*

- *If her hair weren't grey,*
  would I have viewed her as more agile and innovative at work?

- *If she was a man having children, would I then have considered him for*
  this international assignment?

Online design version

This *Framing Perceptions* Inclusion Nudge is as relevant to use in online and telephone interactions as in-person. Biases are also triggered by hearing a voice, the pitch of the voice, and the speed of talking.

You can make a little experiment with yourself; if you cannot see how people look in the online setting, then look them up afterwards to see how they look and pay attention to what kind of perceptions your mind made up – often you'll be surprised. Based on these new insights you can make some great Flip Questions. Give it a try.

Impact

The impact of asking Flip Questions to yourself is obvious when you ask them, because whenever you can answer *'yes'* to your questions, you will often experience some kind of trigger. It can be an emotional trigger, such as surprise or annoyance, or it can be a physical trigger where you feel some reaction in your body, for example in your stomach or your pulse increases. These triggers are your enablers to change your perception and react and behave differently in the moment instead of blindly following your unconscious instinct.

In our work as change makers, Lisa and Tinna have trained and enabled thousands of people worldwide in how to make and use Flip Questions. Of all the enablers we spread, this simple technique is the one most people apply in their daily interactions and in their evaluation and decision-making processes. When it's possible for us to follow up to measure how many use Flip Questions is been 70-80%. We always encourage people to write down their Flip Question (this improves memory) and also to share them with each other. In our sessions, they write them on sticky notes and make a poster with all their examples, so they can learn from reading each other's.

Authors' Comments & Behavioural Insights

We have asked ourselves Flip Questions for decades and it has become obvious to us that this kind of Flip Question will always be necessary to ask because regardless of our knowledge about bias and our expertise about how to mitigate bias, our biases continuously play out in our daily interactions.

Over the years we have been practicing self-compassion because answering Flip Questions is like holding up a mirror in front of yourself and you see things you didn't know about yourself. And the worst thing to do, is to blame yourself for being pre-judging and beat yourself up mentally. As shame researcher Brené Brown states, if you allow shame or denial to take control, then your mind will close down for learning, curiosity, and change. So, instead embrace what you see, make a positive reframing by praising that you noticed your bias and that you get a chance to change your perception and behaviour in the moment. *Embrace it – then you can change it.* We also ask many Flip Questions to other people and the result is always new reflections, interesting conversations about stereotypes, implicit norms, and un-reflected patterns of judgement. In the beginning this will have to be a conscious action, but eventually it will become a new habit, something you do automatically.

Why it works: behavioural insights

Flip Questions work because they **function as triggers** that help us see something that we are blind to. When **seeing and feeling** our own biased thinking, it can help us change our unconscious thought processes and our behaviour, in the moment. Flip Questions work because they are an active cognitive process of imagining the world from another vantage point. This is called perspective taking, which research has repeatedly found to decrease prejudice and stereotyping.[81] That way our biases are not running the show. We need to combat the common notion that by simply being aware of our biases, then this can change them from influencing our behaviours and decision making. We need to help our own brain change perception in the moment to undermine the negative influence of bias. Flipping perspective is an effective way to ensure detachment to maintain objectivity in evaluating people, issues, and perspectives. **Detachment** means the ability to step back to see the bigger picture and act on it.

Publicly Available Resources

You can learn more about Flip Questions and some of **Tinna C. Nielsen's** personal stereotypes in her **TEDx Talk** *Nudge Behaviour for A More Inclusive World*
https://www.youtube.com/watch?v=VggAqa0xOwM

INCLUSIVE

Undermine the negative impact of unconscious biases instead of focusing on awareness

Structured Scoring of 6 Qualifications

The Challenge

As leaders we all know the importance of selecting the right person for a job, and also how difficult it can be to get this right. Even when we know that our intuitive judgements are often flawed, we tend to believe we can dismiss first impressions of people and rate their fit for a position solely based on facts about their attributes and merits. The challenge is how to make a structured fact-based evaluation and still use our intuition.[82]

Anywhere you have to make evaluations and selections (of people, ideas, products, services, etc.), we need to make sure to de-bias the process. Nobel Laurate **Daniel Kahnman's** factual interviewing and structured scoring process[83] is a very impactful approach to mitigate intuitive judgements and improve the quality of the evaluation and decision. The founder and CEO of Applied, **Kate Glazebrook** and her team including **Diana Rocha** and **Andrew Babbage** have also shared a similar structured approach with us. We describe these below and have supplemented with other structured approaches.

The Inclusion Nudge

Evaluate candidates for a job based on 6 independent qualifications. Score each qualification separately on a 1-5 scale. Choose the candidate with the highest total score.

Purpose: Design the talent selection process process for objectivity and reduction of influence of biases to focus on merits and potential.

How To

See below on how you can make your own version. As you read through this, keep in mind that this Inclusion Nudge begins with identifying the qualification criteria for the position (now and in the future), and these should be the foundation for the job description, job advert, application process, interview guide, evaluation of the candidate, as well as the selection process.

❶ Prepare
Version 1: Kahneman's identification of qualifications
Select 5 to 6 traits that are prerequisites for success in this position. Choose traits that are as independent from each other as possible (technical proficiency, reliability, communication, leadership, and so on). You have to be able to assess these reliably by asking a few factual questions. Make a list of such factual questions for each trait.

Kahneman found that obtaining as much specific information as possible about the interviewee's life in the candidate's normal environment is the best predictor of a match to the job. Frame questions about the past and present; their interest in sports, activities, frequency of interactions with friends, how punctual they are in work and studies, etc. Do not make judgements about the candidate's future adjustment to the position.

Version 2: Applied's work-scenario questions
Come up with 'the what': 5 to 7 things that a person needs to be able to do on the job and be specific. Convert these into work tests or scenario-based questions. You can use these as part of the application process, instead of a traditional application. A few examples are:

"It's your first week on the job and you're new to the local area. You've been told that your first priority is to build relationships with the community. How do you spend the week?"
(looks for interpersonal and stakeholder management skills)

"Imagine you have an opportunity to pitch to work on the biggest challenge facing the public sector. What challenge do you choose and why?"
(looks for strategic thinking and public sector understanding/interest)

The team at Applied has found that work-related tests have the highest predictive validity. Applied recommends telling the interviewees upfront that you'll be taking them through a structured interview based on the scenario-based questions which could feel a little wooden, but that it's designed to help them shine.

❷ Interview and evaluation (in both versions 1 and 2)

Collect the information on one trait at a time. Keep the same order of questions in all interview to ensure candidates aren't unfairly discouraged when one question/task is more challenging than others. This will also help with comparison.

Scoring immediately and individually reduces judgemental errors. Try to do it as you go, or at least as soon as you can when the candidate leaves. You can help yourself by always leaving time between candidates to score. Scoring each trait before you move on to the next one. Do not skip around. Score on a scale of 1 (weak) to 5 (strong), or however score ordering happens in your culture.

Make sure each of the members in the recruitment panel make the rating by themselves before sharing with each other to avoid group conformity.

❸ Selection (in both versions 1 and 2)

Add up the scores and select the person with the highest score (even if you like another candidate better).

Use a template for this, because it gives an option to rate the traits in batches for each candidate.

Review trait 1 for all, then trait 2 for all, and so on. This way you avoid rating based on comparison to stereotypes.

Create a template by adding the names of the candidates (vertical columns), and the traits (horizontal rows) after all the interviews and scoring is done. See an illustration on the next page.

EXAMPLE STRUCTURE AND SELECT THE ONE WITH THE HIGHEST TOTAL

Screening criteria Traits/qualifications SCORE 1-5	Candidate A	Candidate B	Candidate C	Candidate D	Candidate E
1. Technical proficiency Factual questions	2	2	4	5	3
2. People development Factual questions	1	2	4	5	3
3. Participatory decision making Factual questions	5	5	5	4	5
4. Xxxxxxx Factual questions	4	3	4	2	3
5. XXX Factual questions	5	5	5	3	4
TOTAL	17	17	(22)	19	18

The template and image created by Tinna C. Nielsen

Impact

Kahneman tested this method when he was working in the Israeli Defence Forces early in his career and set up an interview system for assessing the personality of soldiers to make the right match with various positions.

The procedure improved the outcome from previous interviews where intuition had been dominating. The sum of the rating system predicted soldiers' performance much more accurately (not perfect, but much better).

Kahneman and the interviewers also used a version that added intuitive judgement. After the rating of the candidate, the interviewers would close their eyes and imaging the candidate as a soldier, and this also turned out to add value. But it only had an impact after the disciplined collection of objective information and structured scoring of separate traits. The lesson learned was do not trust intuition but do not dismiss it either.

The team at **Applied** is in the process of testing all of these elements as part of their technology-based solution. Part of this is also testing the impact of one-on-one interviews versus panel interviews based on research suggesting that successive interviews with different members of the team are better than panel interviews. This is largely because they mitigate the risk of **groupthink** on the part of the reviewers. More contact is probably also better for getting a representative sample of the candidate. And if you do multiple interviews, you can shuffle the order of who sees whom and when, allowing you to mitigate **ordering bias** that can influence scores (like being more generous to the first few, or kinder after a terrible interview).

Authors' Comments & Behavioural Insights

Why it works: behavioural insights

This approach works because it mitigates the **'halo effect' bias** that influences any kind of evaluation of people (such as letting one small positive experience spill over into our overall evaluation). Extensive research shows that halo effects are most likely to occur when people employ rapid, automatic processing (system 1) but it disappears when processing more deliberatively (system 2). This is consistent in various everyday situations.

Research findings also show how good or bad **moods** can influence people's tendency to rely on irrelevant information when **forming impressions**. Positive moods increase halo effects and negative moods promoted a more **systematic processing style** which eliminated halo effects.[84] With this structured approach, we can avoid that mood influence.

Scoring each part separately is critical to improving accuracy and objectivity. Beside mitigating the halo effect, it also helps avoid the **peak-end effect**, which predisposes us to remember the peak and the end of an experience and brushes over the rest of experiences. We are less likely to recall the collective experience or the other moments beyond the peak and the ending.

Making a structured evaluation and decision-making process is an effective and simple way to undermine the negative influence of bias instead of focusing on being aware of our own biases.

We encourage you try out various versions of this. As we have experienced many times when experimented with this kind of structured scoring approach, it is always a surprise to realise how different the members in a recruitment committee perceive and rate the candidates. And these differences have given some fascinating insights about each other, created curious conversations when exploring each others views and perceptions, thus given ground to get to know each other better in the group. This has always strengthened inclusive collaboration in the group. And without doubt, this is important for making inclusive talent selection. Give it a try. .

INCLUSIVE

Undermine the negative impact of unconscious biases instead of focusing on awareness

Colour Code People to Ensure Meritocracy

The Challenge

When we as leaders promote other people, we often think we are being objective. However, affinity bias (an unconscious pull towards people who are similar to ourselves) takes over. We tend to prefer people we know better than those we don't. This is further complicated by the influence of stereotypes more than merit as we evaluate other people. When **Stephen Frost**, the CEO of Frost Included, was working with a leadership group and they were rating talent for readiness for promotion, he noticed biased patterns. This is what he designed to address this challenge.

The Inclusion Nudge

Colour code people when evaluating their performance and potential as part of a people calibration process.

Use a colour for various diversity metrics: man, woman, introvert, extrovert, ethnicity dominant in headquarters, minority ethnicity, long tenure, short tenure, and other.

Write the name of every candidate using the assigned colour and add to one of the three categories: 'ready now', 'ready in 1 year', and 'ready in 2 years'.

Identify patterns in colours and categories together.

Purpose: Helps leaders to see potential biased patterns, implicit norms, and stereotypes, such as 'men ready now', 'women ready in 2 years', and 'extroverts ready now', 'introverts ready in 2 years', and other patterns that may emerge.

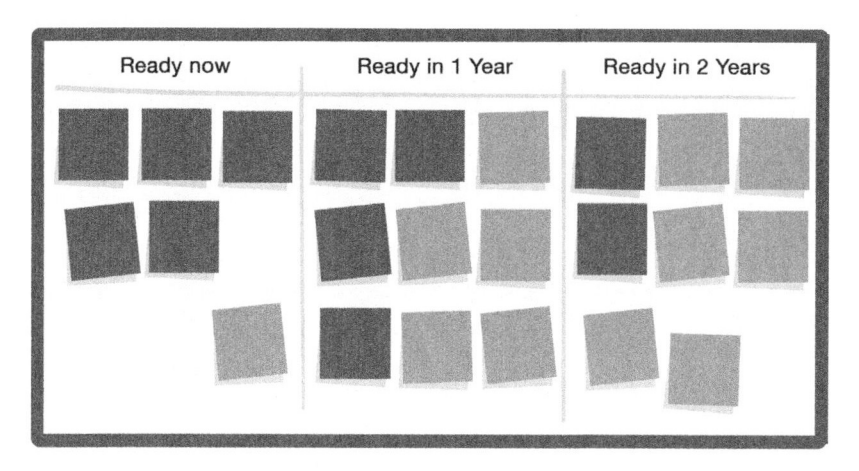

Image created by Christina Hucke

How To

1 Set up the room with three columns on a whiteboard, three flip charts, or three posters on the walls.

2 Instruct the members of the promotion committee or leaders to place their candidates in the three buckets of 'ready now', 'ready in 1 year' and 'ready in 2 years'.

In the original version of this design, the committee members were invited to write their candidates on the whiteboard where men were written in blue and women in green. Blue is stereotypically male and green is associated with 'go' or 'proceed'. This can also be done by using coloured sticky notes.

3 Identify the patterns based on the colours in the three categories.

4 Then, attribute relevant data to the names, such as 360 feedback, performance review feedback, sales, KPIs, etc. to make a fact-based and merit-based evaluation.

5 Talk about the difference and improved balance in men and women being ready now and in 1 or 2 years by applying facts.

Impact

Stephen shares that when the committee saw the results, they were quite shocked because all the people in the 'ready now' category were blue (men) and most of the 'ready in 2 years' were green (women).

The impact was immediate in that promotion committee members could see the impact of their bias. There were women and some men in the 'ready in 2 years' category with better KPI's than those who were in the 'ready now' category. It was a visual representation of suboptimal decision making. Some people were shocked, some felt validated, and some were at first defensive, but it gave everyone a shared understanding of the problem. This then allowed the team to discuss why candidates were where they were and what they wanted to redesign in the process to increase meritocracy.

This process design also prompted some difficult conversations about affinity bias, objectivity, and the skills required. And it did lead to an increase in women being promoted over the three years that this process was applied. Some changes were immediate, such as with 'in the moment' re-evaluations of the promotion decisions. However, the major changes happened year 2 onwards when people knew what was coming and would take pre-emptive action, for example when realising that someone was objectively better and placing them in a different bucket.

Overall, this was a positive change, says Stephen. This process became the default and was accepted as a good check-and-balance design against bias and to improve the meritocracy of the decision-making process overall.

This design also removed the pressure from the diversity protagonist as a 'lobbyist' and moved them into a process of 'facilitator' where the leaders or committee members were debating amongst themselves rather than challenging the process of making the system more diverse and inclusive.

Authors' Comments & Behavioural Insights

This can also function as a motivational intervention, what we call a *Feel the Need* Inclusion Nudge, if you need to ensure buy-in from from other leaders in your organisation to make this an integrated part of the evaluation and decision-making process about who to promote. Here's how to do that.

Create a *Feel the Need* Inclusion Nudge to get buy-in

The participants in the evaluation process start by writing the names of their candidates on similar colour sticky notes and add those to the three categories. Then, ask them to write the names of their candidates again, but this time on different coloured sticky notes; one colour for men and one colour for women, and then add the names again to the three categories next to the others. Do it again for introvert and extrovert (or some other dimension such as nationality, age group, etc.) and add to the three categories next to the two other patterns. You might be in a situation or position where you don't have the power or mandate to ask this of the leaders. If this is the case, then you do it yourself by simply putting one colour sticky notes with the names of men and another colour with the names of women. Ask them *"What patterns do you notice?"*. In this way you can visualise several biases and patterns at the same time and this will be a major eye-opener for them and motivate for them to support implementing this *Process Design* Inclusion Nudge.

Authors' Comments & Behavioural Insights

Why it works: behavioural insights

Visualisation is critical to be able to see clear patterns in complexity. It reveals intricate structures that cannot be absorbed in any other way. It helps the human eye to discover unimagined effects and for us to challenge our imagined realities.

Colours have a functional meaning, in terms of a driving factor for behaviour and perception, when they are detected and encoded by the visual receptors and subsequently processed by its nervous system.[85] Such processing enables what is commonly called **colour perception**.[86]

We can apply learnings from surgery, where the use of **colour cues** has become an important strategy in surgical planning and intervention with the use of visual interface technology for image-guided surgery. Image-guided surgery uses images taken before or during the procedure to help the surgeon navigate. The goal is to augment the surgeon's capacity for decision-making and action during the procedure.[87] Colour is strategically added to images at various stages of the process. In this kind of augmented reality by colour, guidance is provided directly on the surgeon's view of the patient by mixing real and virtual properties of human tissue and organs. Visualisation by colour in this context means translating image data into a graphic representation that is understandable by the surgeon and to convey important information.

In other words, colour is exploited in this context to make the invisible visible, and for helping make critical decisions as swiftly and as safely as possible during interventions, as well as during any kind of evaluation and decision making.

Colour coding is a technique you can use in several of the steps in a talent selection process, as well as in other decision-making processes, such as idea pitching, idea generation, innovation projects, and much more. It's so simple, yet so powerful.

Publicly Available Resources

To understand the importance of visualising data, **Hans Rosling** is one of the most impactful advocates. He has given several TED talks on the importance of this. In his 2006 TED talk, he makes a strong case for animation and visualisation of complexity for us human beings to get the facts straight. Together with **Ola Rosling** and **Anna Rosling Rönnlund**, he has coined the term Factfulness and co-founded the organisation **Gapminders**. They share for free innovative digital tools for visualisation of data, such as animated bubble charts and Dollar Street, in order to make a better world based on facts. It is worth exploring how these could be used in for examples decisions about talent, promotion, succession planning, and more.

INCLUSIVE

WHAT & HOW
I'll make sure to undermine the negative impact of unconscious biases instead of focusing on awareness

INCLUSIVE

Seek out diversity
instead of homogeneity

How Diverse Is Your Network Inner Circle?

The Challenge

We all have a group of people that we seek out for advice when we face an important decision or have a difficult problem to solve. These may be peers across the organisation or professional contacts outside of the organisation. This inner circle of our network usually consists of not more than 10 people and could also be described as our professional (though unofficial) advisory board.

Most of us tend to seek help and advice from others who are very similar to ourselves. Research shows that we have a strong tendency to seek advice **not** from the most **competent** people within our network or organisation, but rather from the people that we like the most.[88] The consequence of this, unfortunately, is that too many people end up with very homogeneous advisory networks. And the more important our decision is, or the bigger and more complex our problem to be solved is, then the larger the need for diversity amongst the people we trust.

If we want to become better at innovative thinking and decision making, we need to make sure that we have a lot of different skillsets and perspectives in our strategic inner circle. If we do not, this may end up having severe implications for our innovative potential as individuals and organisations. Here is an Inclusion Nudge designed by **Susanne Justesen**, who is an Innovation Diversity Advisor with Innoversity in Denmark, to address this challenge.

The Inclusion Nudge

Do a quick assessment of the 5 'go to' people in your network. Identify similarities or differences between their characteristics and your own, such as age, function, gender, nationality, geography, company, and others.

Those people with 4 or more similarities to you will be crossed off the list. After this, most people often have only 1 or 2 people left on their list, because most people have a preference for 'similar others'.

Purpose: Helps to look at your inner circle in a new way, by taking a closer and different look at the people that you tend to seek out for help, advice, and input on challenges in your professional job, revealing whether you tend to seek your input amongst similar others or amongst different others.

How To

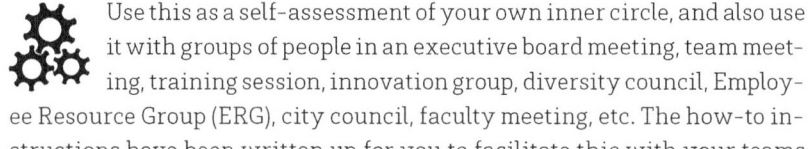

Use this as a self-assessment of your own inner circle, and also use it with groups of people in an executive board meeting, team meeting, training session, innovation group, diversity council, Employee Resource Group (ERG), city council, faculty meeting, etc. The how-to instructions have been written up for you to facilitate this with your teams and with a group of leaders.

❶ Preparation
Create a template with six (or more) horizontal rows and a header row and six vertical columns. The vertical columns can have the following header titles *but you will customise this to your context, these are for your inspiration*. Give each participant a handout with the template on it.

→ Name
→ Organisation *(internal/external)*
→ Gender
→ Educational background
→ Age (a similarity is 5 years +/- from your age)

- → Geographical work location
- → Skin tone/race/ethnicity
- → Work location *(headquarters, country, remote office, etc.)*
- → Function
- → University/educational institution
- → and other you find relevant

You can call the assessment something like:
Who do you seek out for advice or input?

❷ Facilitate

First, ask people to think of five people whom they like to seek out for help and advice on important professional problems, challenges, and decisions (these people may be inside their organisation and/or outside and they may be known through professional and/or personal connections). Ask them to write the five names on a blank piece of paper.

- → Instruct the participants to write their own name in the first row on the table and write their own characteristics (their name, name of organisation, gender, education, age, geographical location, etc.).

- → When they have filled out the first row with their own characteristics, then instruct the participants to take the five names which they just wrote on the blank piece of paper and insert these five names below their own name, in the first column of the table.

- → Then, they take each name and fill out the row, while comparing their own characteristics with the characteristics of each person, based on whether they are different or similar. If they share the same characteristics, just make a line in the relevant table cell (-). For instance, if you belong to the same organisation, have the same age, educational background, etc., then, you just mark the space with (-). If you are different, write the difference (for instance, there is an age difference of 4 years or a geographical distance of 75 km, etc.).

- → When they have done this for all five of their most important 'go-to people', instruct them to look at the table and see if any of them have four or more of the same characteristics, which are marked on the table with line (-). If anyone on their list does, then instruct them to cross out the names of these advisors.

❸ Debrief

When you instruct them to cross out the names of the very similar people, this is a very strong nudge. When they do this, many say that this feels *"painful"* or that they don't want to do this. Explain that the reason you have asked them to cross out those particular names is that the likelihood of these people to be able to tell you anything that you did not already know, or provide you with perspectives that you could not have come up with yourself, is very slim. So, when you seek out this person for help, maybe you should ask yourself whether you are maybe more in search for support by someone who will agree with you. Good advice is much more likely to come from someone who is different from yourself. Tinna used this network assessment for many years and over the years adding steps to enable participants to take action to change identified patterns of homogeneity.

→ Instruct participants to also look for patterns of homogeneity in the vertical columns, such as do all 5 in the inner circle have the same gender, nationality, etc.
→ Instruct the participants to discuss in small groups what each of them will do to challenge patterns of homogeneity. Instruct them to use peer coaching by asking questions for reflection and not give advice.
→ Instruct each of them to identify people they already know who can challenge some of their patterns. Write down the name of that person and commit to reach out to that person next time advice is needed.

Design variation: multiple purposes

Scott Ballina 🐾, previously with the Bill and Melinda Gates Foundation, and now the Senior Director for Diversity, Inclusion, and Belonging at Citrix, was inspired by this Inclusion Nudge when it was published in the 2nd edition of *The Inclusion Nudges Guidebook* (2016). He has used this in his work in these organisations, and has adapted it to fit each context. In his current organisation, he calls this exercise "Shopping an Idea". Scott has expanded to use this also with an external customer analysis focus, highlighting patterns such as

→ 'How wide is our customer group?'
→ 'Who might we have missed?'
→ 'Who are on our teams presenting to customers?'

Another design change that Scott has made is to simplify the handout by having it as a blank table. He requests that the participants complete the vertical column header titles with demographic categories, which he **prompts** them by showing several examples. Each participant selects the ones relevant to them and writes that in the table for use in the assessment. This increases a sense of ownership on the outcomes revealed in the review. While in other times, he has used a hybrid model with having a few (2 or 3) demographic categories already identified and leaving the others open for the participants to define. This helps to make sure the organisational priorities in their inclusion strategy are included in the network analysis and helps to bring the strategy to *"real life"* experience. It also avoids participants skipping over the ones that might feel *"uncomfortable"* or that they don't agree with. The hybrid model also allows for a global-local customisation to blend the already determined organisation-wide topics with the different locally relevant ones.

Online design version

Do this *Feel the Need* Inclusion Nudge in a virtual way by having the participants do their network mapping as pre-work to the meeting. Then, they bring in their filled-in template to this online session. In the session, you instruct them to mark the similarities and do the crossing out. Follow the How To instructions. Use a poll question to reveal the shared patterns of how many people they have left on their list.

Impact

We (the authors) have used this Inclusion Nudge in multiple settings, organisations, and countries. And the pattern is the same. Most people are really surprised to see how many people in their inner circle are very similar to themselves. Therefore, this is a powerful nudge for more diversity and inclusion by having people think differently about who to actively seek out for advice or input. Most people are surprised to have only a few people left on the list, revealing that there are only a few people that can potentially provide them with different perspectives than they would not have been able to come up with themselves.

This is an eye-opener and motivates people to challenge an often-hidden behavioural pattern. It also motivates them to actively reach out to other people they already trust and who can provide them with more diverse perspectives. The majority of the people who have done this assessment, report that they have changed their own behaviour and diversified their network inner circle.

Authors' Comments & Behavioural Insights

You can make many design variations of this *Feel the Need* Inclusion Nudge. It can also be used in people evaluation and selection processes, and to make our unconscious preference for similarity visible in the process. Instead of assessing your network inner circle, you assess the candidates' characteristics that you have nominated to help identify bias for similarity. Often the same kind of similarity dominates in the evaluation of qualifications and performance. This is what hiring managers started doing (by themselves) in an organisation, where **Tinna C. Nielsen** was previously Head of Inclusion. The hiring managers would add characteristics that influenced them in hiring and based on insights that they had about their own individual biases and preferences (could be height, clothing style, body size).

Why it works: behavioural insights

The reason it works to visualise the patterns in your network inner circle is because human beings have a tendency to believe more in what we can see. Actually, we are reluctant to believe factual evidence when we cannot see it. That's why it important to make the patterns of our behaviour and preferences visible. We need to see to know and **seeing is believing**. First of all, we need to see the bigger picture and patterns of our many individual actions or unconscious preferences. Second of all, what you cannot see, you do not change. It is crucial to target the unconscious mind to help ourselves and other people see and make us feel the need to change anything.[89]

We recommend that you use this network mapping yourself – how does your network inner circle look? Use it on a regular basis to check for progress. This is a simple way to help yourself and others seek out diversity instead of homogeneity.

INCLUSIVE

Seek out diversity
instead of homogeneity

Maximum 70% Homogeneity Team Composition & Target

The Challenge

It is often a challenge that teams are not composed in ways that ensure the right mix of diversity, people, and skills. In this way, we miss out on greater potential and innovation. Research[90] by Susanne Justesen, who is an innovation diversity advisor and the Founder of Innoversity in Copenhagen, shows that too much **homogeneity** (sameness) in a group directly impacts performance. This was measured based on the groups' ability to solve problems, make decisions, reach their deadlines, maintain their budgets, and not least of all, their overall economic performance. The direct link between performance and group homogeneity was the strongest when the homogeneity of nationality, gender, or age group (generation) did not exceed 70% in the groups measured. That is, group performance became negatively impacted when more than 70% of group members had the same gender, the same nationality, and/or belonged to the same age group. Research on releasing the innovative potential in teams by the London Business School found that 50:50 on gender had the biggest impact.[91]

Another challenge is the way we set targets for diversity in our organisations. We tend to focus on the minorities and gender diversity. Often, the connotations of target setting, such as 30% women in leadership, are of a moral character with associations of *"nice to have"*. Unfortunately, this triggers unconscious perceptions that diversity is a *"women's issue"* based on bias thinking that women should be fixed and that women are hired only because they are women and not because they are competent.

To benefit from diversity in our organisations, it's important to change these stuck perceptions about diversity and to change the way we compose teams.

Diversity must have connotations to performance and innovation (this is a resource perspective) and not to minority and women. Perceptions can be reframed by setting targets based on facts about high-performing teams and diversity. Thereby, turning the diversity agenda away from being a *"nice to have"* towards rather a *"need to have"*.

Here's how **Tinna C. Nielsen** addressed this in her former role as Head of Inclusion, Diversity and Collaboration in Arla Foods.

> **The Inclusion Nudge**
>
> Set a target for the maximum similarity of various demographic factors.
>
> Set a team composition target for how to compose high-performance teams:
> A 'Maximum 70% Homogeneity' team target.
>
> → Max. 70% of team members with the same **national/ethnic background**
> → Max. 70% of team members with the same **gender**
> → Max. 70% of team members from the same **generation**
> → Max. 70% of team members from the same **educational/professional background**
>
> **Reframe the targets to be about reducing homogeneity.**

Purpose: Reframe perceptions as a means to achieve more diversity in teams without having to talk about diversity. Communicate diversity targets as team composition targets for better performance and to align with leaders' existing performance aspirations. By communicating your diversity targets this way, you avoid triggering perceptions that diversity is about women or minorities. Avoid communicating targets such as *"30% women"* because it fosters *"fix-the-women"* perceptions.

How To

Cluster gender with other differences
Avoid associations of women being *"the problem to fix"*. Couple gender with other differences, such as nationality and age. Also, watch for patterns of the use of *"gender"* but actually referencing only women and not the full spectrum of gender.

Differentiate the target
Be realistic in accordance with the current pipeline and hierarchical levels. For example, the Executive Management Group and Business Group's Top Leadership teams have to reach the objective in all four factors. Other leadership teams and employee teams (including project teams) have to reach the objective in at least two factors and more if possible (if in the available recruitment base). The above example was the team objective set in Arla Foods. Add other characteristics depending on the specific reality in your situation (such as a bias towards specific universities). Set the target according to your pipeline. If you have access to more diversity, then set it as 'Maximum 50 % of the same ...'.

Create composition assessment tool
Use a template (a simple one-page spreadsheet) to assess the percentage of the dominant gender, nationality, generation, educational and professional background, and/or other criteria in your context. Add the number of members in the team (for example 10 people), then add how many team members out of 10 have the same nationality (don't write the nationality), how many have the same gender, how many out of 10 are from the same generation), and so on. This current team composition assessment is important to use in hiring situations to make informed decisions and increase the quality of the selection process. When you have two equally qualified candidates, look at the assessment to decide if you need a man or women to reduce the percentage of the dominant gender in order to achieve maximum 70 % homogeneity. In some cases, you might have to choose between reducing sameness in gender or generation and you will end up with a higher percentage of gender because you made a decision that generational diversity was more important for the team and the tasks at hand.

The objective does not have to be mandatory nor linked to bonuses to work. Create motivation and buy-in from leaders by showing research results and internal data that demonstrate the correlation between team composition and performance.[92] Create a **follow the herd** reaction by showcasing that the majority of 'similar others' are reaching this target, such as by communicating that *"7 out of 10 teams in your unit have achieved the target and are comprised of a mix of talents to increase innovation"*.

Design Variation

There are many ways diversity targets can contribute to alter perceptions. Here is an example of gender targets we spotted in a press release from the law firm Baker McKenzie[93] in June 2019. This 40:40:20 example illustrates how you can broaden gender goals to be more inclusive across the gender spectrum.

→ 40 % women
→ 40 % men
→ 20 % flexible (women, men, or non-binary persons)

Impact

The performance diversity measures behind the 'max 70 % principle' relates to teams only (when there is direct collaboration amongst the group members in question). Research shows that when the prevalence of demographic factors, such as gender, generation, and nationality, are set at a maximum of 70 % on a team, then the performance is better. The profit margin is on average 3.7 % higher in diverse teams versus more homogeneous teams and than in teams with a higher prevalence of the above factors.[94]

By changing targets for the representation of demographic diversity in teams and the perception about inclusion and diversity in Arla Foods, the conversation changed to be predominantly resource and performance oriented. This discourse change was driven by those who had participated in the inclusion and diversity (this was not the title) learning session (which was a bottom-up change movement). Leaders expressed their explicit support for such target setting because it resonated with performance and innovation. One leader created a tool spreadsheet to measure the composition of the current team and used this to make a fact-based and informed selection in hiring situations. The leader shared this tool with the human resource department and they shared it across the organisation.

Leaders in Arla Foods used the objective as a guiding principle in recruitment, restructuring of teams, staffing project teams, and composing work groups. And none of the leaders were being held accountable or forced to reach this goal. Instead, they worked on achieving it because it made sense for them, and that's why the reframing worked so successfully. They reported positive group dynamics and better performance in the diverse teams.

Authors' Comments & Behavioural Insights

Why it works: behavioural insights
The focus matters

Setting such a target is reframing the perception of diversity as an end goal, and is instead creating a focus on reducing 'sameness' as a crucial enabler to achieving better performance and innovation. When focusing on this, you focus on the **'meaningful destination'** which is innovation and high-performance for most managers and project leaders and that **focus steers** our behaviour.

The framing matters

With this framing you avoid triggering some of the negative feelings many people unconsciously **associate with words** such as *"diversity"* and *"gender equality"* which can be a loss of privileges, being with people who are not my in-group, feeling insecure, harder work (due to more communication), sharing power, and much more. Without mentioning *"diversity"*, this framing helps to achieve more diversity.

If a message is framed like this
*"Of one hundred patients who have this operation,
ninety are alive after five years"*
then we perceive that as a comforting message.

But if the same facts are framed like this
*"Of one hundred patients who have this operation,
ten are dead after five years"*
then we would be alarmed and perceive that as negative.

This means that it matters a lot how we present the data, including how we set targets and communicate about them. This is the case in all issues, because framing shapes our mental associations, and thus perceptions and behaviours.

The psychologists Amos Tversky and Daniel Kahneman identified the impact of framing and published their findings in the article *The Framing of Decisions and the Psychology of Choice*.[95]

The order matters
The order of the demographic characteristics you list in the target is important because the first information creates an **anchor** in the thought process. So, if you want to change a very common perception of *"diversity"* being about *women and minorities* to a perception of diversity being about all of us, make sure to list, for example, age or nationality in the beginning, instead of starting with gender (which many perceive as only *"women"*). Put gender in the middle of the demographic characteristics listing.

The pioneering research[96] on anchoring was done by Amos Tversky and Daniel Kahneman in the 1970's and is still highly relevant, especially when it comes to reframing perceptions.

INCLUSIVE

Seek out diversity
instead of homogeneity

Difference as Criterion for Selection, Not De-Selection

The Challenge

There is a well-known unconscious bias (called the "mini-me") that can influence recruitment decisions, whereby we tend to prefer candidates similar to ourselves. This bias can prevent selecting the best candidates and benefiting from the recruitment of a diverse mix of thinking styles, capabilities, and life experiences. This is how **Janina Norton**, Head of Employee Engagement at AXA Investment Managers helped hiring managers change their perception on candidates and diversity and is inspiration on how leaders can do this with their fellow leaders as well.

The Inclusion Nudge

As an integrated part of the selection of candidates at the beginning of the recruitment process, have recruiters ask the hiring manager questions to prod 'difference' as a selection criterion.

The recruiter asks the hiring manager questions as on the next page.

After the interview, check for patterns in 'differences' among candidate, manager, and team.

> "What attributes or traits do you not have, that it would be ideal for the new candidate to have?"
>
> "How could this candidate's detail-orientation style supplement your [the manager] big-picture orientation?"
>
> "What traits would be useful for the candidate to have that don't 'fit' with the current team, which might mix things up and create more diverse perspectives?"

Purpose: Demote preferences for similarity in the evaluation and decision-making process by reframing the perception of difference from being a burden to being a resource, and thus promote behaviours that support that happening.

How To

Ideally, all leaders, recruiters and hiring managers within an organisation should have some understanding on the impact unconscious bias on decisions during recruitment.

1 Before advertising, the hiring manager and recruiter meet to discuss the approach that will be taken to recruit. There is usually already a formal set of questions for this conversation, to discuss what attributes, skills, and experience the ideal candidate will have. An additional area of questioning is added to this briefing questionnaire. These questions frame 'difference' as an asset for the team, manager, and purpose.

2 After the interview, check for patterns in differences among candidates, the manager, and the current team. Revisit the original briefing document. Raise questions and discuss whether the selected candidate has different traits than the team currently has which would benefit the team and the work.

❸ Refer to specific difference identified as valuable by the hiring manager: *"Does this new candidate deliver a different style of working, a different set of life experiences, or a way of thinking that is currently missing within the team?"*. It makes the individual candidate's differences a conscious criteria for selection, rather than the unconscious criteria for de-selection.

Impact

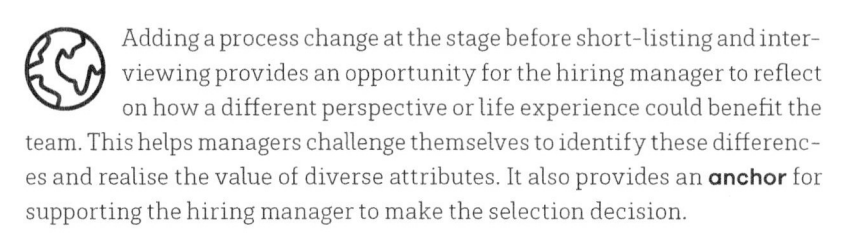

Adding a process change at the stage before short-listing and interviewing provides an opportunity for the hiring manager to reflect on how a different perspective or life experience could benefit the team. This helps managers challenge themselves to identify these differences and realise the value of diverse attributes. It also provides an **anchor** for supporting the hiring manager to make the selection decision.

Authors' Comments & Behavioural Insights

We recommend that to further strengthen this Inclusion Nudge that you make visible the patterns of 'de-selection' arguments and 'selection' arguments from previous recruitment processes. Do this using a pre-designed template or list. Managers make marks on the template to ensure that their own patterns are visible. View and discuss possible implications of the patterns.

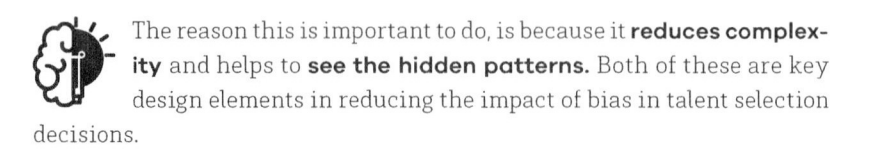

The reason this is important to do, is because it **reduces complexity** and helps to **see the hidden patterns.** Both of these are key design elements in reducing the impact of bias in talent selection decisions.

INCLUSIVE

> **WHAT & HOW**
> I'll make sure to seek out diversity instead of homogeneity

Implement redesigns of practices, processes, & systems
based on facts & behavioural insights

Anonymise People to Focus on Merit

The Challenge

Often, the screening and evaluation process for a new hire or promotion is influenced by such visual impressions as the layout and style of a resume or application, as well as by implicit associations of gender, skin colour, age, and other biases. This is also the case in the analysis of assessment results, in interviews, and in the selection processes. To ensure a fair process and selection of the best candidates, it is crucial to design the process to be as objective as possible.

Unconscious bias awareness and intercultural intelligence are not enough to make the screening and selection process objective. It is necessary to implement steps that help the brain make better decisions and reduce the negative impact of biases, and thus challenge the behavioural drivers of the status quo, mindless choice, and confirmation bias.

The Inclusion Nudge

Make candidates anonymous in the evaluation and selection process by removing as much identity data as possible in applications.

Purpose: Ensure a focus on merit and qualifications by removing visual and identity information that may trigger bias and detract from objective decision making in various stages within a talent selection process.

How To

There are different opportunities to integrate this intervention as part of existing talent attraction and hiring processes and systems. Some of these are described below.

The process can be fully automated, such as in this example.

→ In the recruiting technology-based system, demographic identity factors, such as gender, age, name, address, and photo, are not revealed to the recruiter and the interviewing team during the early screening process steps. Only when the candidates for interviewing have been selected is identity information given, if at all as in some cases the identify data still may not be given then depending on other bias mitigating design steps in the full talent attraction process.

The process design can also be fully manual, such as it was done in this example. When resumes come in, have an assistant manually remove names and geographic information, assigning each resume a number. This is how many hiring managers did it in Arla Foods where **Tinna C. Nielsen** was the Global Head of Inclusion. They came up with this themselves after having experienced another *Feel the Need* Inclusion Nudge. Also, at a Danish film institute, when Tinna worked with the reviewers of applications for film funding, they asked their assistant to cut out all identity data from paper versions of the applications.

→ Let the applicants know about this process design. Write on your talent attraction website, application platform, and in the job description that applicants should remove identity data from the application and CV and submit a separate page with this information.

→ Instruct your assistant or colleague to hold on the separate identity page. You request it when you have chosen the candidates you want to meet for an interview. **Tinna** does this in her organisation Move the Elephant for Inclusiveness. Also, we noticed on **Stephen Frost's** (CEO of Frost Included and a contributor to *The Inclusion Nudges Guidebook*) company website that they have done this in past job postings.

Multiple ways you can do this

You can also anonymise when selecting members for internal councils, communities, panels, etc. In a technology firm in Denmark it was decided to build an internal community of champions to master and spread the Inclusion Nudges change techniques in their organisation. The (former) CEO was to select a diverse group of 12 leaders in the organisation based on their application to be part of this community. **Ulla Dalsgaard** (one of the Diversity Leads) gave him a list of 50 applicants without any identity data (anonymous). The CEO said *"How am I supposed to choose when I cannot see who they are?"*. As soon as he had said that, he realised that this was exactly why he needed help with selecting the team objectively and not in a biased manner.

Blind skills assessments.

Kedar Iyer, from the organisation GapJumpers, shared that they worked with a technology company to apply blind skills assessments (anonymising the candidates' assessment results) for specific roles in their talent attraction process. Anonymising the candidate on the CV is not enough based on some research findings[97] and GapJumpers' experience. Instead, their focus is on the assessment testing and results reporting to be anonymised within the talent attraction process.

Request anonymised shortlist of search agency

Another option is when you use search agencies to help you find candidates, and you ask them to deliver a list of diverse candidates, remember to require (make this part of your formal contractual agreement) of them to anonymise candidates on both the long- and short-lists. **Lisa Kepinski** (Founder of Inclusion Institute) did this when she was an internal head of inclusion and diversity in a multinational. This was a two-step process. First, it was necessary to set the contracted terms that the search agency would deliver gender diverse candidates (the percentage target varied based on the role and function, such as at least 30% females for IT and 50% for finance). Only a few people had visibility to verify that the list met the agreed upon targets. Secondly, when presenting these to the recruiting lead and hiring manager, the candidate list and information was anonymised.

Impact

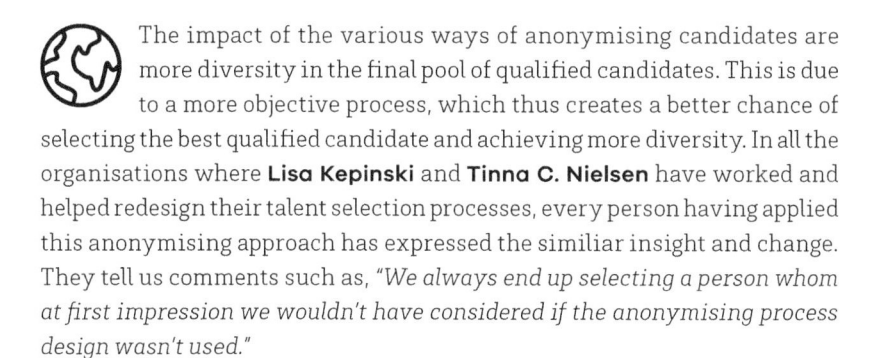

The impact of the various ways of anonymising candidates are more diversity in the final pool of qualified candidates. This is due to a more objective process, which thus creates a better chance of selecting the best qualified candidate and achieving more diversity. In all the organisations where **Lisa Kepinski** and **Tinna C. Nielsen** have worked and helped redesign their talent selection processes, every person having applied this anonymising approach has expressed the similiar insight and change. They tell us comments such as, *"We always end up selecting a person whom at first impression we wouldn't have considered if the anonymising process design wasn't used."*

What **Ulla** did was to apply the anonymised screening Inclusion Nudge to help them to choose objectively from the list of candidates according to the qualification criteria. She had also helped the CEO realise the importance of anonymising the applicants and *feel the need* to make this change in the selection process.

This internal community was diverse in terms of gender, tenure, age, function, and professional background. They went through a full Inclusion Nudge Design Learning Lab with **Tinna**. The community has since been assigned several corporate tasks by the executive team and additionally other teams in the organisation are asking for their assistance.

Kedar shared that in an organisation that they worked with the anonymised skills assessment resulted in 20% more minority candidates selected to interview for software engineering roles and 32% more minority candidates selected for data analytics roles. The process also included candidates from more diverse backgrounds than the established norm, with 40% of those selected for interviews being self-taught and/or educated at boot camps rather than the traditional university education path. This 'alternative' education path had not previously been a criterion to advance in the talent selection process. They also found that the blind skills assessments reduced the total time to hire by 26%. So, not only was the talent pool more diverse and the process fairer, but it was also more efficient.

In **Lisa's** example, there were two key learnings from the experience. The first was that a level of oversight was needed to ensure that the search agency actually delivered on the expectation for a gender diverse list. It was hard for them to shift their past ways of sourcing candidates. At that time, her organisation was one of the search firm's very few clients that *required* this of them. Other clients talked about wanting it, but did not put in place serious contract targets for them to deliver on it. Their first results with Lisa's organisation didn't match up to their expectation. This is why a step of having an internal reviewer of the candidate lists (Lisa and/or a member of the talent attraction team not involved in filling the role) was put in place before going onward in the process. Initially, this review happened with every list, and later it fell to spot checks after the search agency improved to meet the expectations (contractual agreements). Another learning was that often the search consultant would present the lists in two formats, one written and then a briefing discussion with the hiring manager. The latter allowed for the influence of bias by how the search consultant referenced some candidates over others. While the process design of having the candidate list anonymised was working, the next step in the process skewed the hiring manager's decision making. So, we eliminated the briefing discussion and only used the written lists. There was an increase in women who were interviewed after this process was put in place.

Another example of this design having impact is from a technology & engineering multinational (who shares this anonymously). They applied the approach in selecting members for their internal Diversity, Equity, and Inclusion (DEI) Council in the U.S., after having read about it in the past edition of *The Inclusion Nudges Guidebook*. They were surprised, and pleased, with the unexpected results of who was selected to serve on their DEI Council. This *Process Design* Inclusion Nudge bought in wider diversity than they had anticipated and was a reminder of how their own views could have influenced who was not considered if they hadn't put the anonymous process in place.

Authors' Comments & Behavioural Insights

Why it works: behavioural insights

Anonymising people works because it avoids the **halo effect** to influence the evaluation of a person's merit. The halo effect is an error in reasoning based on one single trait, often irrelevant, that creates a 'halo' of the overall impression and perception of that person.[98]

The term halo effect was coined in 1920 by psychologist Edward L. Thorndike. It's based on Thorndike's observations of military officers 'ranking' of subordinates. Before communicating with their subordinates, the officers ranked them based on character traits, which included leadership ability and intelligence. Their **positive and negative perceptions** were based on unrelated traits that had to do with physical impressions. For example, a tall and attractive subordinate was perceived as being the most intelligent. He was also ranked as overall 'better' than the others. Thorndike found that **physical appearances** are the most influential in determining our overall impressions of another person's character, which can result in either positive or negative perceptions. The halo bias can have negative consequences on your ability to think critically about a person's other traits and abilities.

The halo effect does not only influence evaluation and selection in hiring situations, but also when it comes to ideas, investments, pitching, and also in schools. For example, there's some evidence that perceived attractiveness can lead to higher grades in school.[99] Another study found that teachers assigned higher grades to the essays by students with **common, popular, and attractive first names** versus essays by students with rare, unpopular, and unattractive names.[100]

A need for a whole system de-biasing process

There is a compelling need to design to reduce the influence of bias within your processes across the whole system, not just one part of the system, such as only with recruiting by anonymising applicants.

This was illustrated by the recent discrimination legal case with the Boston symphony orchestra. They were one of the first institutions to implement anonymous interviewing decades ago, by implementing anonymous music auditions behind a screen and as a result increasing the number of women by 40% and also changing the ethnic make up of the orchestra. Yet, they were sued by a leading female member of the Philharmonic for being significantly underpaid (the case was for more than $200,000 in unpaid wages) to her male counterparts in the orchestra. This was because the Boston symphony had not ensured that its whole system had been redesigned to lessen bias effects. Further reports have shown that while now women comprise about 47% of musicians in symphony orchestras in the U.S., there are very few female composers who have their music performed by symphony orchestras in the U.S. During the 2019-20 season in the U.S., 90% of the music to be played is from male composers and only 10 % from women composers, with *"the numbers for composer of color even more dismal"*.[101]

Designing to reduce bias needs to happen across all processes that work within the whole system. When you are implementing this design in your talent selection process, look at the connected processes across the total organisation and apply the same de-biasing and nudge design approach.

Implement redesigns of practices, processes, & systems
based on facts & behavioural insights

Default as 'All Qualified' & 'Why Not'

The Challenge

Mental tendencies and biases can work against making good evaluations and decisions about people, solutions, ideas, roles, and much more. Often this is due to the starting point (the default and the anchor) of that process. The challenge is that qualified, sometimes even the best, solutions and people are de-selected. When it comes to talent evaluations in organisations, this is critical because it has a significant influence on the successful achievement of the organisations's strategy and purpose. Yet, bias impacts evaluation of performance with a tendency to rating recent performance more highly than past performance. People tend to opt-in on people who fit the implicit norms and have similarities to themselves. They reflect the status quo and so feel safer.

Sue Johnson, a former global head of diversity & inclusion at Nestlé and now an advisor with PwC Switzerland, noticed a pattern in her past company during talent discussions. People who were seen as different from the norms, who were also usually the same people labelled as 'diverse', were talked about as *"Should we take a risk on this person?"* or *"Is this person a safe bet?"*. These people were often not similar to the decision makers or deviated from the implicit norm and stereotypes of the 'typical' employee for that role. This resulted in unequal evaluations, and thus unequal opportunities for career opportunities, compensation, and a loss of performance potential in the organisation. Sue implemented a simple change in the process design to shift the default of the discussions.

The Inclusion Nudge

Make the default in evaluations and selection processes "All are qualified".

Change the argumentation default to "Why not?"

Purpose: Shift the anchor of the thought process to promote more objective evaluations and work against biased tendencies in decision making. In most workplaces, when deciding who to select for a project or promotion, leaders ask, *"Who is qualified?"* and then, they argue *"Why?"* the candidates they find more qualified are ready. That is a very biased process. With a default of *"All are qualified",* they have to argue *"Why not?"* (opt out) instead of *"Why?"* (opt in).

How To

Implement this in successor evaluation meetings *('All are qualified')* or performance-calibration meetings *('All start with the highest rating').* Apply this default in idea pitching processes, innovation processes, hiring and promotion, and any where else where you have several options to choose from.

When it comes to people, for example when evaluating each candidate for a job, it's important to search for facts about why this person would not be qualified and why this person would be qualified. Make sure the evaluators challenge each other on the assumptions about the candidates. Make it fact based.

Impact

Nestlé used this *Process Design* Inclusion Nudge to focus on promoting gender balance in succession planning. They changed the default in discussion about who was ready for a promotion or bigger responsibility to 'All are ready now'. This broadened the pool of candidates being evaluated, it shifted the perspective on what it means to be ready, reduced bias in the decision-making process, and promoted more objective evaluations.

Authors' Comments & Behavioural Insights

We believe that this kind of default design has the potential to reduce biases about nationality, race, ethnicity, gender identity, sexual orientation, abilities, personality, communication style, age, etc., thereby increasing diversity broadly in leadership and talent pipelines.

We also see that this can be applied to other decision-making processes to ensure that a more open perspective is activated rather than a limiting one driven by our mental fallacies and biases. For example, in idea pitching sessions for funding, investors, and internal resource allocation.

Why it works: behavioural insights
Changing the **default** has been used in many situations with positive effects and multiple outcomes.

One well-known example is with organ donation programmes shifting the **default** from citizens having to register **(opt in)** to a default where all citizens are registered and free to **opt out.** In the countries where people have to opt in, very few people register despite their intentions to do so (it's too complex a choice and too effortful). In the countries where the default is automatic registration the majority of citizens stay in the system. This works because it **reduces complexity** and makes it **effortless** to do what we intend to do. Very few people *opt out* because that is an equally complex choice and as effortful as *opting in.*

Using **default** nudges to foster more inclusion, changes our thinking from an unconscious choice based on bias to a conscious search for facts. Selecting the best qualified candidates requires that we view a diverse pool of candidates, but most people have difficulty opting in on diversity, such as a person who is not like the majority, does not fit the implicit norms in the organisation, is a minority, does not look or communicate like those already working in that position, etc. This requires more effort and involves complexity in choosing. ***Opting in* on someone we do not recognise as a 'fit' is difficult. On the other hand, *opting out* on a qualified candidate (when**

having facts that counter bias) is an equally difficult process even when they don't fit the norm.

With the *'all are qualified'* **default** we make sure it does not require a lot of effort to opt in on **'outliers'** (those perceived as having some form of difference from the norm) and we make it less likely that they are going to opt out on a qualified candidate due to diversity or not an obvious cultural 'fit'. This will help ensure the best qualified and more diversity is selected.

To learn more about the research on default design, read the Inclusion Nudge **'FLEXIBLE WORK' AS THE DEFAULT IN THE JOB REQUEST FORM** (→ page 90).

Implementing this kind of redesign of processes and systems based on behavioural insights is the most effective way to make inclusion the default and norm in our organisations and communities.

INCLUSIVE

Implement redesigns of practices, processes, & systems based on facts & behavioural insights

Neutral Observer in Evaluation Meetings

The Challenge

To help ensure a lessening of bias in talent discussions, designing the talent assessment discussions to include ways to capture bias in action and address it in the discussion can be powerful de-biasing process step. This can help to bring greater objectivity and fairer talent assessments for the organisation and the employees. This is how **Charlotte Sweeney**, the founder of Charlotte Sweeney Associates, has been working as a neutral observer in organisations' talent discussions.

> **The Inclusion Nudge**
>
> Use 'neutral' observation and feedback from the observer (plus a video recording) as an integrated part of the talent review process

Purpose: Capture and reveal when bias is occurring in talent discussions, and address in the meeting to ensure more objective assessments and selection of candidates.

How To

Apply this Inclusion Nudge for more inclusive evaluations when it is relevant, such as during talent reviews, succession planning, and promotions period. Having a neutral observer as part of any evaluation discussion can add value, regardless of that being about talent, research grants, peer reviews, innovation projects, funding, investment, film subsidies, or other situations.

❶ Prepare

Ensure understanding and agreement from all participants to video record the meeting.

To get support for having a neutral observer participate and to record, you might need to design a motivation nudge to get buy-in from all the participants. They might need to see that bias influence evaluations and decisions, for them to see the need for this kind of process design. You can get inspiration in the *Action Guide for Motivating Allies*, with 30 Inclusion Nudges for this purpose.

Call out the role of the neutral observer is purely to observe throughout. Share there will be questions from the observer after the discussion process finishes and a review of some of the footage.

❷ During the meeting

The observer turns on the recording (pre agreement by participants before the meeting).

During the meeting the observer writes notes about the conversations, about biases, preconceptions, stereotypes, patterns in ways of talking and words being used.

When the decision is made, have a break, and the observer makes an overview of patterns emerging from the notes.

❸ Debrief

Once the decisions have been made, ask the participants to reflect on these types of questions:

"How easy was it to come to a consensus about who would be promoted?"
"Do you feel that you and the team have been fair and equitable throughout the process?"
"Were there any words and phrases used for the different candidates that you discussed?"
"Could any biases have slipped into your discussion?"

Then, replay parts of the video for all in the room to see and hear the discussions and to also watch their body language on the screen. Continue the discussion about what was happening throughout the meeting after they watched some of the footage. Ask them to call out any patterns noticed and could these have impacted the promotion (or other topic) decisions made? Review the talent decisions again.

In the post-discussion debrief, before reviewing the video, Charlotte says that all felt they had given the candidates a fair review and that the right people were going to get promoted. None of the attendees could recall any examples where they had spoken about the promotions differently.

Charlotte then shared a couple of examples that she had observed, including:

*"You referred to one male as committed to his role, not ready for the promotion yet but at risk of leaving if you didn't promote him this year. You also spoke about a female candidate who you thought was 90% ready this year but that an extra year would make sure she was **really** ready. What was the difference between those two decisions?"*

"You referred to one person who was excelling at their job and had outstanding performance ratings for the last four years; however, you didn't know if you should promote this person because the new manager in that area has a 'thing' about people without a degree. How did that shape your thinking?"

While there were a number of other examples that she shared to gain their views on their decision-making process, many couldn't recall those specific aspects of the discussions and were not sure they had actually been said. Although this process did take some time to complete, it was clear that many in the room had not consciously been aware of some of the comments or body language until they watched the video.

Online design version

This can be easily be done in online meetings. You simply follow the same instructions. The observer can report back in real time to the group verbally, or by the whiteboard, or by using the chat feature. The report back needs to be direct quotes (word by word) what was said. Or the observation can be done in two parts by using the recording feature in the online meeting platform. First conduct the discussion, then do the debrief by replaying for all the recording of the meeting and have a facilitated discussion that engages all to call out where biased may have cropped up in the talent review as described in the how to steps. This can actually have an even stronger impact than just saying it to people because 'seeing is believing'.

Impact

Charlotte explains that it only takes a few minutes for all attendees to feel comfortable and forget about the recording. After watching the playback of the video, they felt they needed to review some of the decisions and discuss again. Different decisions were made in a few cases. Feedback from the attendees was hugely positive. They felt more aware of the impact unconscious bias had on their everyday decision making. As a result of the exercise, the process of recording the discussions and reviewing the videos as a decision-making team was introduced throughout the promotions process for a specific region and recommended for delivery in other regions.

Authors' Comments & Behavioural Insights

Why it works: behavioural insights

This process intervention is powerful when it is an integrated part of evaluation and decision making discussions. Here are some of the behavioural insights explaining why this works.

Being seen
The observation itself can have an equally important impact as the feedback afterwards. The fact that we know we are being **'seen'** can in itself change our behaviour, meaning that it's not solely by watching the recording the change happens. Research has shown how individuals modify their behaviour when under observation (being 'studied' and 'singled' out),[102] and another study showed how pictures of eyes on a piece of paper increased ethics and moral behaviour.[103] The pictures of eyes functioned as **salient cues that primed** the unconscious mind and fostered specific behaviour.

Seeing is believing

The recording of the discussions is powerful because it holds a mirror to leaders' spoken and non-verbal communications. This can motivate change because seeing our own behaviour on video, shifts perception and increase awareness of hidden behaviours. This has an impact on motivation to make changes because **seeing is believing**.[104] It's much better to *show* than *tell*.

Seeing the gap

This is impactful because leaders and evaluators can see the gap themselves. By first asking them about their own perception of their fairness in the process, most will answer in accordance with their self-perception more than based on how fair they acted in the process. The gap is realised by then afterwards showing them the facts about their actual (biased) behaviour. Seeing this gap can in itself help alter behaviour in the long-term and not just in that one meeting.[105]

Implementing such a redesign of the evaluation process based on behavioural insights about the difficulty of being aware of ones biased during discussions, is a valuable contribution to ensure that decisions are based more on facts and less on assumptions, stereotypes and personal preferences.

As a leader you have the power to suggest this for the next discussions and meetings where important decisions will be made.

INCLUSIVE

WHAT & HOW
I'll make sure to implement redesigns of practices, processes, & systems based on facts & behavioural insights

Verbalise support & actions for inclusion, diversity, & equality instead of silent consent

'If Not, Why Not' Accountability

The Challenge

Most organisations with an inclusion, equity, & diversity program want to increase diversity among staff at all levels. Efforts include widening the talent pool, engaging with specialised search agencies, improving employer branding campaigns, establishing internal targets with senior executives reviewing for progress, leadership development training, and mentoring. Despite these actions, progress remains slow in most organisations. The intentions are good, but often actions simply reinforce the existing demographic structure. Clearly, we need an approach that involves the unconscious mind, as this is pivotal in maintaining the status quo and resisting change.

The Inclusion Nudge

'If not, why not?' reporting to executive manager when the decision is to NOT recommend a candidate from underrepresented (minority) groups for a position or a promotion.

Purpose: Reporting to senior leaders makes sure hiring managers are being held accountable for their responsibility to hire and promote the best qualified and achieve more diversity and inclusion.

How To

Make it part of the hiring and promotion process for hiring managers to report *"if not, why not"* to their executive leaders.

Most organisations have intentions and targets for increasing the diversity of their leadership. If a person from an under-represented group that is part of these targeted goals was not among those recommended for hire or promotion when a senior-level opportunity opened up, then the manager would be required (based on prior agreement from the CEO/executive leadership team) to report *"why not"* (facts) to the executive management team.

This accountability is further strengthened by requiring the selection committee to find as many facts as possible that would disaffirm or affirm the decision not to hire or promote a person from an under-represented group. Looking for facts that can explain why the candidate was not selected, as compared to the candidate that was selected, can counter biased decisions and confirmation bias.

When **Lisa Kepinski**, Founder of Inclusion Institute, was an internal inclusion and diversity leader in a multinational, there was a similar approach employed that required a 'skip level manager' discussion (so with your manager's manager) if a candidate from a minority group was not hired.

A process review was conducted where the steps of the selection decision making were examined and questioned. In some cases, this occurred prior to the final decision and making an offer to the leading candidate. It resulted in some candidates getting a second look and if not given the role, they were often referred for another internal role (it was a period of rapid hiring with many open roles). In other cases, it was done post-hiring decision making. Insights from this post-review were then integrated into the hiring process, such as understanding more about the questions asked of all the candidates' during the interview and how to improve it through more behavioural-based questions.

Another way to improve judgement and decisions is to ask for facts and data that confirm or disconfirm a decision. This is crucial and should be an integrated part of all decisions because often the data sample used in decision-making processes are biased. The facts (pros and cons) should be reported to the most senior leaders as well.

This was an important learning coming out of the explosion of the NASA Space Shuttle Challenger in 1986. The investigation reveals that the engineers had presented a biased data sample of when the test flight failed but not of all the test flights including when succeeding. And no one had asked for the disconfirming data showing the opposite of the data sample. Based on this, the decision was made to launch the flight with fatal outcomes.

When making decisions based on data being presented, that data has been selected by one or more people, and in that process, they have deselected other data. You want to have access to that. Create a decision-making process where the default is that every time data is presented, it will show data for both the positive and negative pertinent; 'when it works' and 'not works' or pro and con or positive and negative. Make sure the facts and data that shows the whole picture is the foundation for the decision.

Authors' Comments & Behavioural Insights

Why it works: behavioural insights

The awareness of the procedure itself, knowing you have to report and are held accountable, is **priming** for a change of perception in the unconscious mind and for a more reflected thought process. This can have more influence than the actual reporting. When we know that others see us (see what we do and don't do), it influences our behaviour. Knowing that we will be held accountable for how we have made our decision, and what facts and data we used in our decision-making, makes us more conscious about what we base our decision on.

An interesting demonstration of the **priming effect**, was created by researcher Melissa Bateson at a university.[106] The staff paid for tea and coffee and did this by dropping money in a box on the table. A list of prices was posted on the wall above the box. For a period of ten weeks, she added a new image without explanation. Five weeks with flowers and five weeks with eyes (at the top of the price list). No one commented on this change. But the amount people paid did change. They paid almost three times as much in the 'eyes weeks' as they did in the 'flowers weeks'. This means that being watched prodded the unconscious mind to change behaviour. In this case, the effect occurred without any awareness.

In this Inclusion Nudge of 'if not, why not reporting', they are aware of being watched and that has a similar priming effect. **Priming** refers to a psychological manipulation were the presence of a stimulus (the 'prime') alters subsequent behaviour of the people experiencing the stimulus. This can be words, visuals, colours, eyes, changes in the environment, and much more. Priming has been well documented in both cognitive and social psychology, and behavioural economics.

It might well be that the reason 'if not, why not reporting' works is not due to the priming effect, but due to the effects of the **social environment**. One fundamental feature of decision environments in social and organisational settings is the need for individuals to account for (or justify) their judgements to themselves and others. **Accountability** is a critical **norm enforcement mechanism**[107] that influences judgement and evaluations. This is being reinforced with 'if not, why not reporting'.

It is important to look for patterns of unintentional spin offs and negative implications, such as political correctness or hiring diversity candidates to merely meet targets or unsupported hires of minority candidates (where they are not properly onboarded or supported in the role).

This is not only relevant to use when it comes to making decisions about who to hire and promote, but also when it comes to making decisions in general. For example, this inclusive design can be useful when it comes to development and decisions about people, consumers, ideas, technology, markets, city planning, communities, social welfare and more. There is no limitation to where this is relevant.

Imaging the effect of local politicians requiring of investors and architects, who are building apartment housing, that they have to include a default component of social community (to increase belonging and combat loneliness and social isolation). If they don't account for that in their permission application, then, they will have to comply with the 'if not, why not reporting'. Just imagine what effect that could have. Or when ideas are selected and de-selected, this kind of accountability reporting might influence how ideas are being judged, and open up access to more diverse ideas being put forth by knowing that they will be considered. Imagine the impact of 'if not, why not reporting' built into product and services designs to ensure accessibility by all people rather than based on a potentially biased view of who is the 'normal' person.

Having to account for our choices of who and what we select and deselect is a way to be explicit about supporting diversity, equity, and diversity in actions – both as organisational and individual leaders.

If it's not the norm in your organisation to ask this of leaders and managers, ask this of your team and colleagues. You can make it the default and norm.

INCLUSIVE

Verbalise support & actions for inclusion, diversity,
& equality instead of silent consent

Show the Hidden People by Reversing the Numbers

The Challenge

It's often a challenge to use data, for example from employee engagement surveys, in a way that motivates change. Often, these numbers are shared in meetings or leadership sessions and discussed in terms of *"Are we on track?"* or *"Is there room for improvement?"*. The data and numbers distance us from the lived reality and from the people that are hidden behind the numbers.

So how can we, in simple ways, make the numbers count and use the data to trigger change?

In an organisation where **Tinna C. Nielsen** was working with executive leaders through her change-organisation Move the Elephant for Inclusiveness, the Head of Human Resource was sharing the results of the annual employee engagement survey. They were celebrating that *"65 % of employees feel empowered and have opportunities to grow"*. Here is what Tinna did spontaneously, when she was on the meeting agenda right after this 'celebration'.

> **The Inclusion Nudge**
>
> Re-frame the perception by reversing the numbers to show the hidden facts.
>
> Ask:
> "How many people are working here?"
> Ask: "How many is 35% out of the total number of employees?"
>
> Then say:
> "If 65% feel empowered and growing, then 22,000 (35%) of your employees do NOT feel empowered and do not have opportunities to grow. That is a lot of talent to miss out on!"

Purpose: Reverse the numbers to change perceptions to see the full picture and see the hidden people behind the numbers and also the consequences.

How To

When highlighting that the annual employee survey shows that *"65% of employees feel empowered and growing" (for example)*, then engage the leaders, your team, or your colleagues in doing the math. Ask the questions as described above. Then ask them, *"Do you wonder what opportunities you/we are missing out on?"*

Do this in the moment – every time you hear someone highlighting the numbers of *"how great we are doing"*, then you reframe their perception by calling out what the numbers are not showing – highlight the opposite numbers to illustrate how many people that are not a part of that *"great"* number.

Make sure you involve the people you want to influence in doing the math because it activates their mind and they will remember better and also take more ownership – it's their employees and their responsibility.

Impact

When the leaders realised that 22,000 of their employees did not feel empowered and growing, something interesting happened, says Tinna based on her experience as the facilitator of change. Their facial expressions changed, they looked surprised, and the energy shifted.

Tinna has designed and facilitated leadership development for a couple of decades, and this was, by far, the most energised 4 hours with executive leaders that she had ever experienced. Executive leaders are exposed to many kinds of facilitators and consultants, and it's not unusual that they implicitly express some kind of fatigue in the beginning of a session, such as *"here we go again"*. But flipping the data helped them see a hidden issue and feel an urgency to change this and make sure to be inclusive of the talent of those 22,000 people as well. This was confirmed by numerous leaders after the session. They were curious and eager to engage and learn about the micro-strategies and enablers on how to make the changes happen effectively.

Authors' Comments & Behavioural Insight

Our experience is that over the years of applying the Inclusion Nudges change-approach, we (Lisa and Tinna) find ourselves in situations where we automatically notice an opportunity to reframe a message, a question, data, situation, or challenge, and that we can do it in the moment without a lot of time to consider how to or when to. We are convinced that this is due to practicing over a long period of time and just trying it out. It feels extremely empowering to be able to call it out in the moments and almost intuitively.

Why it works: behavioural insights

It's a powerful way to verbalise support for inclusion, diversity, and equality without having to use these terms or call out 'I am an ally'. Reversing the numbers to show the hidden people is much more powerful because it motivates the unconscious mind to take action. It works because it helps us see an issue in a new perspective and it triggers the **loss aversion bias** (we want to avoid losing or missing out). You can influence many people to be more inclusive. Our hope is, that you will give it a go.

I N C L U S I V E

Verbalise support & actions for inclusion, diversity, & equality instead of silent consent

Valuing Staff Contributions for Inclusive Culture

The Challenge

? Often inclusion and diversity work in organisations is seen as *"on top of the employee's day job"*. This mental model of it being *"extra work"* and not related to one's formal role can result in employee involvement in inclusion and diversity programmes not being valued by managers, who may fail to see the wider corporate citizenship contributions that employees can make to benefit the business and people. This mindset also does not recognise that inclusion is behaviour that is everybody's daily responsibility.

One way that this gets overlooked is by not including employees' contribution to inclusion and diversity initiatives and how they contribute to an inclusive culture in their annual performance review and appraisal process. This under-valuing and under-recognition of inclusion and diversity-related contributions by employees has a negative impact on the sustainability of these initiatives, the needed change, and also impacts employee engagement.[108] Here's how **Veronika Hucke**, Founder of D&I Strategy & Solutions, & **Lisa Kepinski,** Founder of Inclusion Institute, have shared with organisations on how to do this.

The Inclusion Nudge

Insert a prompter question within the performance appraisal process.
(insert in the IT system for performance reviews)

Purpose: Ensure that employee contributions to an organisation's inclusion and diversity strategy are recognised and discussed as the default and norm, and thus being perceived as everybody's responsibility.

How To

Within the performance appraisal process, include standard questions for all employees when they write up their accomplishments and development plans that cover their efforts beyond what is typically described as "their day job". Design the questions to cover both the formal company-related activities, **plus** other informal, relevant activities and actions.

The intent is to ensure that the performance appraisal process includes a wider view of what are "valued" employee contributions to the business, workplace, or community and meaningful options for learning and skills development. The question, as default in the process, signals to employees and managers that the organisation recognises and rewards employee involvement and that such engagement is an advantage for the organisation. This shifts the perception of inclusion and diversity being a 'nice to have' to instead being core to the business and a viable investment of employees' time, which is recognised and rewarded by the organisation's managers.

Examples of questions:

"In addition to your formal objectives, identify contributions you have done to the make our workplace place more inclusive."

"How have you helped support making this a great place to work for all employees?"

"How do you make sure the diverse knowledge of your team members is being included to make stronger decisions and achieve our priorities?"

While this *Process Design* Inclusion Nudge example is related to inclusion and diversity, the questions can be written in a broader way that encompasses a wide range of employee contributions to the organisation in other areas such as Corporate Social Responsibility, community volunteerism, employee and company events, customer-facing product launches, graduate student recruiting fairs, representing the company by speaking at events, and other special projects – all of which are aligned with the organisation's business strategy but are outside of the formal role description or what is typically perceived as one's "day job".

Impact

By integrating such questions into the formal performance appraisal process, it provides a wider view of employees' contributions towards supporting the organisation's goals and culture. It also communicates to employees and managers that inclusion and diversity are seen as important to the organisation. Often when being asked how many people are working on inclusion and diversity, respondents will only consider colleagues that are formally tasked with the role. In that context, it is important to highlight that each employee has a role to play to create an inclusive culture. In this way verbalizing support and taking action for diversity, equity, and inclusion becomes the norm.

I·N·C·L·U·S·I·**V**·E

> **WHAT & HOW**
> I'll make sure to verbalise support & actions for inclusion, diversity, & equality instead of silent consent

Empower people and groups
instead of disempower

The Speech Bubble Intervention

The Challenge

All organisations have issues with unacceptable behaviour, some more and some less, but harassment, bullying, and discrimination are a part of human behaviour. How it plays out in organisations has a lot to do with the culture and leadership, as well as the procedures in place to deal with this. The problem is that this kind of behaviour is often hidden and silenced. A lot of people do not have a voice in the sense that they don't have the opportunity to share their experiences or it can be too vulnerable to share their personal experiences of being treated poorly.

We need to get access to the voices of people in order to surface unattended issues and to change cultures of unacceptable behaviour, because those in privileged positions who have not experienced it personally may find it difficult to grasp the issue and problem, and thus do not take action.

Personal stories about the impact on personal lives, the community, and/or the organisation are proven as powerful ways to motivate us to listen, see, and engage. But it is rarely possible to put people who are vulnerable in front of other people, leaders, or decision makers to share their stories and to get others engaged in making changes. To address these challenges, **Tinna C. Nielsen**, Founder of Move the Elephant for Inclusiveness, designed what she calls 'The Speech Bubble Intervention' when she was working internally as a global Head of Inclusion, Diversity, and Collaboration. In this organisation, the leaders knew about the issues of unacceptable behaviour because they were informed about the outcome of the annual employee engagement survey. But this knowledge did not get the leaders engaged in changing this nor taking proactive measures on a systematic level. The data had even proved to create distance to the problem. Often the leaders would react to the information by engaging in a discussion about the legal definitions of harassment and discrimination (the rational mind took over). In order to create buy-in and engagement from the leaders and managers to change this, it was necessary to help them see the issues to address these problems by giving a voice to the people who experienced this. This is the intervention that Tinna designed by applying behavioural insights.

The Inclusion Nudge

Display real-life personal experiences from employees of unacceptable behaviour, written in the first-person style, as quotes, in speech bubbles. Decorate the walls in a room with the speech bubbles from floor to ceiling.

Invite the leaders to read them by saying, "Your colleagues/employees have something to tell you." Humanise the numbers; write on a big poster the exact number of [insert your organisation's name] employees experiencing unacceptable behaviour in the organisation.

Reverse the business case by highlighting the losses of not changing the current state.

Picture by Tinna C. Nielsen, from the original intervention

Purpose: Make the voices of *'the people it's about'* heard by people in privileged positions. Help people see hidden issues, show them instead of telling them, help them *feel the need* to change the status quo instead of making them rationally understand with data, and based on this get them engaged in making changes.

How To

This intervention has been designed in a variety of versions since it was first created by Tinna, and it has been used in a lot of organisations, communities, and countries to address many hidden issues. It has given people a voice, it has empowered people, it has engaged people, it has increased empathy and connection, and it has fostered impactful change. This is how the original intervention to address unacceptable behaviour was designed and facilitated for an executive leadership team. This is also how you as a leader can do it yourself or collaborate with others to design and facilitate it. Your target group can be other leaders or employees, committee or community members.

ATTENTION!
Make sure to apply all steps – do not skip any of them. We have seen it go really wrong when applying only a few of them.

❶ Design
Collect real life examples of personal experiences from a diverse and representative group of people experiencing unacceptable behaviour in the organisation. Aim for minimum 40 examples.

ATTENTION!
Do not facilitate this for your team with stories from your team – that's too small a group and too vulnerable for them. Make sure all can stay anonymous and not be recognised. Also, you need many stories to have impact.

Convert each example into **first-person quotes** like, "When my colleagues ..., then I ... everyday I feel ..." Make sure people are anonymised. Merge examples to ensure anonymity.

Write each example in speech bubbles and print them.

Display the speech bubbles on the walls in a room (preferable the room where the target group has their regular meetings – this might help them remember the experience every time they have meetings in the future and, in this way, keep attention on these issues). Make sure to have enough speech bubble examples to cover all the walls completely – you can duplicate the examples to have enough. They have to feel surrounded by the voices of people.

❷ Facilitate
(about 15-25 min) – *see behavioural insights explanations later*

→ Tell them, *"Your* [organisation's name] *colleagues have something to tell you"*. (This sentence is important. Also, use the term commonly used in your organisation--colleagues, staff, employees, peers, associates, etc..)

→ Instruct the leaders to walk around in the room to read the real-life examples of what their colleagues experience on a daily basis in this organisation. The purpose is to make them *feel, not rationalise.*

→ Humanise the numbers, by converting the percentage of people who have experienced this behaviour (from the internal employee survey) into the exact *number* of people. Write the numbers on a big poster like this,
"12 % = 4867 [company name] *employees in our organisation."*

Read this out loud to the leaders/participants and as you read this add, *"… going to work every day feeling miserable and underperforming as a result".*

The purpose is to *show, don't tell.*

→ Make a reverse business case by showing findings from research illustrating the negative implications of this. In the original intervention, research data showing a 30 % decrease in decision-making ability was communicated, along research showing how one person in a team experiencing harassment affects the productivity of the entire team negatively by 12.5 %.[109]

→ Invite the leaders to calculate how much the company loses in terms of people, talent, finance, etc. Numbers and cost efficiently are what leaders are often good at, so make sure to tap into this skill. Make sure you have some suggestions as a backup.

→ Ask the leaders what actions they suggest.

→ Share with them the 2-3 most critical actions to take (not all those that you have in your action plan for this issue). Keep it simple and reduce complexity. The first suggestion should be, *"Send this intervention on a tour in the organisation and start top down with senior leaders."* This was the suggestion this first leadership team came up with and it had a significant impact.

We always recommend that you make sure to follow up with the leaders to learn from the actions they initiate and to help spread these in the organisation or community where you want to see the changes happen. Learning from each other is one of the most powerful ways to learn.

You can apply 'follow the herd' communication if a majority of the leaders take action. Make sure to communicate to the others that *"7 out 10 of your colleagues have done [name specific examples of action]"*. In this way you highlight the social norm, and human beings tend to blindly follow what the majority of 'similar others' do. This is much more powerful than pointing fingers at those who do not act.

Online design version

You can do this *Feel the Need* Inclusion Nudge in a online context. Follow all the How To steps to design. Then, in the meeting send the speech bubble document to participants. This is important to do within the meeting, not before or as pre-work, because the feeling of empathy needs to be triggered in the moment for effect and impact as part of the design. Follow the rest of the How To steps.

ATTENTION!

It's important to read how behavioural insights is a key element in this design. See the Authors' Comments & Behavioural Insights section.

Impact

The leaders who experienced this intervention were shocked by the experiences their employees were sharing and shocked to learn that employees and colleagues were treating each other this way.

That was the purpose of this intervention – to make them *feel the need* to engage in changing this.

This is how the intervention played out. There was complete silence in the room as the leaders were walking around reading the examples. Many crossed their arms in front of their chest, some held a hand on their throat, others over their mouth, some looked surprised, some looked sad, others looked disgusted. After having read all of the examples, the leaders in the room started talking together and they were talking about feelings – which is not common in leadership groups (its often considered a sign of weakness). For some, it came as a surprise how these issues played out in their organisation. Some did not believe all of them; some said, *"This incident must be old – we fixed this years ago"*. One expressed discomfort when he said *"I feel nauseous"*, one said *"I am so sad for our colleagues"*, and another said *"This is going on right in front of our eyes and we don't see this"*, and another said *"I didn't even know, and now I am really angry"*, and another said *"I can hardly breath"*, and one whispered *"I think I might have said some of that too"*.

The result was immediate support. One leader suggested to send 'this experience' on a tour in the organisations *"the other leaders have to experience and feel this – this cannot be told. Let's start with the Supply Chain Board and Human Resource Board together. They need to experience this together to join forces"*. Another leader suggested to add a focus on a 'mentally safe work environment' to the agenda in all leadership team meetings across the organisation along with the existing focus on a 'physical safe work environment' and prioritise to take action immediately. They took the lead and the responsibility for doing this. This also led to leaders engaging the employees locally in coming up with ways to change these issues and promote an inclusive culture. This kind of local activity turned out to be much more impactful than a global policy, action plan, and compliance. This created action and ownership.

So, in the end this intervention led to an inclusive co-creation process together with 'the people it's about'. This kind of participatory change process is what we need much more of in order to create greater ownership of changing our workplaces and communities to be inclusive as the default and the norm.

Here is a trick how to make more impact with this intervention and how to get more people engaged in facilitating this across your organisation. In a global organisation that Tinna has collaborated with for several years through her change organisation called Move the Elephant for Inclusiveness, created a version of the intervention that would make it easy to reuse and send on a tour in the organisation. They literally built an entire wall (see picture below) with the speech bubbles, that they could move and reuse. Now, that's much more efficient than sticking hundreds of separate speech bubbles on the walls and having to take them down again and repeat it all in a new location (and less messy on the walls afterwards).

Picture by Tinna C. Nielsen

Authors Comments & Behavioural insights

We might think that all people turn a *"blind eye"* to this kind of behaviour. In some cases that is true, but research also shows that people in privileged positions are blind to inequality – they are not capable of seeing it.[110] And what you cannot see, you do not change. It is crucial to target the unconscious mind to help all people see and feel, and thus enable people to act.

You can use this as inspiration to address a totally different issue. When you understand the design behind this intervention, you can design and apply it to many different situations. When Tinna designed the Speech Bubble intervention, she was inspired by an example from Chip and Dan Heath's book called *Switch*, where they described how a manager had failed in several attempts to get the executive leadership team to centralise procurement. He succeeded only when he did something unexpected that got them to *see* the need themselves. He had a summer intern collect all the work gloves that were being purchased in all the business units. It was a total of 424. Price tags were then added to the gloves that were the same to show that in one unit it was purchased at 17 dollars while only for 5 dollars by another unit. They put all the work gloves on the conference room table and the executives would pick up the gloves with their hands, look at the price tags, and they quickly realised the need to change the current procurement system. They could see the issue and they felt it. This intervention sparked Tinna's idea to get the executives to *see and feel* the issue of unacceptable behaviour.

If we can get from work gloves to harassment with one such practical example, then only our imagination can limit us. Use all the Inclusion Nudges in this Action Guide to spark new ideas and execute on them by designing them based on evidence about how the human mind and behavioural drivers work.

Why it works: behavioural insights

Several behavioural insights have been applied in this design. Make sure to apply all in your design.

Activate tribal mentality

The first sentence *"Your colleagues have something to tell you"* is designed to trigger the **tribal mentality** 'this is my tribe' and 'I am their leader – I am supposed to protect my tribe'. The effect of triggering our tribalism towards our **in-group** in this intervention is emotional engagement. We listen more closely to our tribe members.

Change the messenger

This intervention changes the **messenger** from being the 'facilitator' to being 'the people'. The messenger is a powerful influencer on our behaviour, and when our **peers are the messenger** it often has a bigger influence on what we do, how we listen, and what we hear.[111]

Trigger empathy and pain

Experience other people being treated badly, discriminated, and socially excluded. It triggers the area of the brain where **physical pain** and **empathy** is located, even when we're not directly experiencing it ourselves. Reading the experiences of colleagues motivates us to want to change this.[112]

Humanise the numbers

Numbers and data and statistics are communicated to the rational mind (system 2) but that is not the mind that makes the changes, that is system 1 and that part of the mind does not care about numbers but about people (it's emotional). That's why it's important to humanise the numbers. The voices do that. As well as when you convert the percentage into an actual number of employees (example: 12% into 4867 [company name] employees). In this way, **feelings of a social bond** are activated.

Loss-aversion bias

When being confronted with losses, such as a loss of the staff's decision-making ability and team productivity, or the threat of losing their identity image as professional leaders (by not having taken action to change this), it triggers the **loss aversion bias** (pain of losing is psychologically about twice as powerful as the pleasure of gaining).[113] The basic principle of loss aversion can explain why **penalty framing** (losing money, performance, business, etc.) is sometimes more effective than reward framing in motivating people.[114] Reversing the 'business case' in this intervention proved to be motivational.

Ownership

Getting the people that you are trying to influence to get engaged, take action, or change behaviour requires that they feel ownership of this. You can create that by asking them to calculate the loss and ask them what solutions they see, instead of giving them an action plan to execute. And also, you can create this by asking them for solutions.

Reduce complexity

For any kind of change to occur it's crucial to reduce complexity. That's why it's important to only communicate 1-3 of the most important steps regardless of you (as the change maker) probably having at least 20 actions lined up in your action plan. Go simple – start small.

The strength of this intervention is that it motivates to take action without controlling the outcome. It empowers *'the people it's about'* to apply their diverse insights and ideas in joint effort with peers and they all own the solutions. Another strength is that the people often realise that they themselves are as much a part of the problem as 'the others', which in many cases has led to mitigation of 'us' and 'them', the **attribution error bias,** and fostered more social cohesion and inclusive culture.

Design variation
Many versions have been designed by change makers around the world for many different purposes. Here are a few examples.

Reduce conflict in a refugee camp
A 26-year-old social entrepreneur, **Daniel** 🐾, in the Kakuma Refugee Camp in Kenya, was inspired by the design of the Speech Bubble intervention to design a variation that could help increase empathy across the various clans in the refugee camp. He designed an intervention to reduce conflict between clan leaders by getting them to hear each other's stories, identify similarities, and for them to collaborate in making improvements in the community.

Align self-perception as the 'good people' in humanitarian organisations
Tinna has worked with international NGOs and humanitarian organisations to help change the culture and behaviour and reduce the psychological phenomenon called **moral licensing**. This is a subconscious phenomenon occurring when we have established a self-perception as 'a good person' that leads to less effort in actually behaving according to standards of moral and ethical behaviour and decisions, such as equality, non-discrimination, and inclusion. Our unconscious mind gives us a moral licence to act opposite of our stated values, beliefs, and intentions – and we don't even notice it happening. Our unconscious mind even uses the self-perception of being morally righteous in one context as justification for acting immorally in other areas.[115] As a result, even organisations on a mission to create a more equal world, better lives for everyone, reduce discrimination, and leave no one behind, have issues with discrimination, harassment, and bullying. The Speech Bubble intervention was designed to show the employees' examples of how their peers *'experience working in the organisation today'* and how they *'wish it would feel to work in the organisation'*. The two kinds of examples were displayed on two separate walls in the room. This was to help them spot the patterns and gaps between *'current state and experience'* and *'aspiration and hope'* and realise the issues that many people experienced. Many were really surprised to hear about specific incidences of internal discrimination, but equally surprised to learn that so many of their colleagues felt lonely and excluded at work.

Spotting lack of purpose in fast growing start up
In a fast growing start-up company, there was an issue with a lack of 'purpose' and the bigger mission of the organisation. At the same time, this com-

pany had to lay off many people. The leaders thought the issues of frustration among the staff were due to the layoffs. To get the leaders to realise that the issue was more about a lack of purpose and direction, **Diane** 🧠, an internal change maker, and Tinna created a version addressing this. They asked them a few questions about their experience of working in the organisation. They asked before the layoffs and after the layoffs. The answers were displayed on separate walls and the leaders had the task of spotting the patterns. The leaders quickly realised what issue they needed to deal with.

Listen to the voices of citizens in city development

In a small city in Denmark, a citizen council had been established to facilitate a change process of creating a more vibrant city centre and public space that would create inclusive communities and interactions. Over time, the 6 members had established themselves as the decision makers of what kind of change was needed and what solutions were the best. The problem was they were not including the perspectives and ideas of other citizens with the result that they were not engaged and no inclusive community arose. Tinna and a group of social architects designed a Speech Bubble intervention that displayed the voices of the citizens, their wishes for their city, their ideas, and their frustrations. This was an eye-opener for the city council members and gave them new insights to work with. It helped them realise the need to change their approach and to loosen up their need to control the process.

Strengthen citizen participatory processes

The Speech Bubble intervention has also proven effective in participatory co-creation processes, for example when public service providers, politicians, city developers, architects invite citizens into the ideation and development stage of a project. This intervention is useful in terms of actually hearing the voices of *'the people it's about'* as described in the example above, but it is equally important to use when it comes to handing over the output of such a participatory process to the decision-makers and policy makers. Unfortunately, what often happens in the handover is that the diversity of perspectives is reduced to one page and a spreadsheet, and poor decisions are made and outdated solutions are reused.

❗ Do not underestimate the impact of helping yourself as a leader and other leaders to hear the voice and stories of 'the people it's about' as part of any decision-making! Empowering people and groups is a prerequisite for making changes. Especially, when it comes to the kind of inclusive changes we need worldwide.

INCLUSIVE

Empower people and groups
instead of disempower

Checklist to Balance In-Group & Out-Group Opportunities

The Challenge

The in-group and out-group dynamic can have profound implications in workplaces on areas such as onboarding newcomers, information sharing, assignment of key projects, visibility, decision making, and promotion. Since we have a strong bias in favour of those that we perceive to be like us, these people become the people that we connect with most frequently. This is sometimes called our 'go-to' people. We tend to trust their input more and interact with them at higher levels than those who are in our out-group. The out-group members are the people who are least like us and with whom we have lower levels of trust, respect, connection, and engagement.

This sorting of people into our in-groups and out-groups happens on an automatic, unreflective level, even when we don't wish it to happen. This dynamic is a key reason why being inclusive of all is a challenge. Inclusion becomes especially complicated when team managers have in-group members on their work teams. Managers may not be aware of the in-group dynamic at play, since they are feeling comfortable when they interact with people who are like them.

All of this will influence the opportunities people in a team have, and often unintentionally result in unequal opportunities to develop, contribute, and advance.

The Inclusion Nudge

Use a customised checklist to identity patterns of inequality and bias as an integrated part of decision making and allocation of work assignments and any other kind of opportunities.

Check for patterns in type of work assignment and identity characteristics of team members.

Make the list transparent and discuss with the team as an integrated part of team meetings.

Purpose: See and realise how the patterns of the in-group and out-group impact access to opportunities for individuals. Use a systemic approach with a checklist to ensure greater equity and leverage all talents.

How To

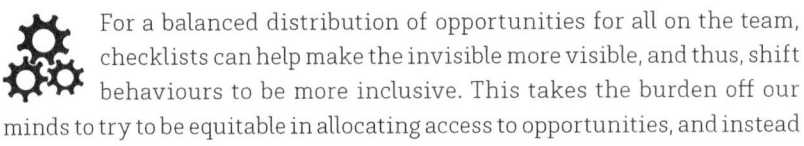

For a balanced distribution of opportunities for all on the team, checklists can help make the invisible more visible, and thus, shift behaviours to be more inclusive. This takes the burden off our minds to try to be equitable in allocating access to opportunities, and instead alters the process to steer decisions more equitably.

The first step is to identify how in-group and out-group dynamics are showing up in a team. Conduct a data analysis study of the allocation of opportunities to each of the team members. This may cover the number and types of projects assigned, amount of time spent speaking both formally and informally, who speaks and doesn't speak in meetings, access to development opportunities, and others. What are the patterns revealed by the audit? If the outcomes are not inclusive of all, then design a checklist to help shift this. Here are three ways.

Version 1: Team work allocation
Dan Robertson 🌐, director at Vercida Consulting, has shared this approach.

1. Each week, managers should chart and track, using a simple diary system, their work allocation decisions, noting:

   → The types of work being allocated
   → The value of the work
   → The name
   → The importance of the client

   Weekly, the manager reviews these decisions and cross-references these to identity and team characteristics, such as ethnicity, gender, age, office location, and other such agreed criteria.

2. Next, share this information with all team members. The manager's decision becomes open to scrutiny from team members. This acts as a nudge towards accountability within work allocation decision-making.

3. Hold a monthly meeting with the team where decision-making patterns are reviewed for possible bias. On identifying any bias, the manager commits a set of actions to correct this over the following month. Team members act as accountability agents to ensure corrections are made.

Version 2: Use checklist to share all tasks
Tinna C. Nielsen, Founder of Move the Elephant for Inclusiveness, and **Lisa Kepinski,** Founder of Inclusion Institute, further expand this checklist technique. If you are a manager or leading a group of people, find ways (numbers, pick out of the hat, alpha or birth order) to rotate tasks and opportunities (speaking roles, responsibilities, note-taking, conferences, etc.) so that everyone gets a chance. Make sure to include both the high-value and low-value tasks so all share the benefits and the burdens across the range of things to be done. Make it the norm to rotate tasks equally and encourage this to become a process used by all. This will help with co-ownership and make the checklist a team norm.

Online design version

For online team meetings, use a checklist. The impact of in-groups and out-groups on a manager's team is even more complex when the team does not always work together in the same location. In a recent global research study, **Veronika Hucke**, Founder of D&I Strategy and Solutions, and **Lisa Kepinski,** Founder of Inclusion Institute, looked at increasing inclusion in distributed teams who do not sit together. With globally nearly 45% of professional employees and managers working at times or always in another location than their team, this is a new reality of how work gets done, which has greatly increased due to the pandemic of 2020.

With geographically distributed teams, care is even more needed to not forget those who are not sitting next to us (a danger of 'out of sight, out of mind'). To lessen this, use a checklist for all team meetings to ensure that everyone has an opportunity to contribute their input on all items on the meeting agenda. This helps to mitigate physical-presence dominance, such as having the team members that you see in person as being the ones who speak most often, are called upon most frequently, and whose ideas are noted the most in team meetings.[116] Design a process checklist for the virtual team meetings with the agenda points and the names of everyone on the team. Tick off as team members contribute per topic. Not everyone may have something to say, but the checklist will be a way to ensure that they are asked for input, rather than having to remember who spoke and who didn't. Also, the checklist serves as a real time data log if someone is dominating the discussion and you can take action to clear space in the discussion for others who have not shared at all or as much.

Impact

Dan reports the impact as *"by documenting work allocation decisions, managers and team members have a record of actual decisions made, and reply less on subjective memory; this process increases openness and transparency with the decision-making process, which we know acts a motivator for behaviour change and fair decision-making. Finally, and most critically, this activity is designed to identify any possible race, gender, age, etc. bias early within the process and, thus, act as a correction mechanism, resulting in a reduction in both short-term bias and long-term bias."*

Authors' Comments & Behavioural Insights

Why it works: behavioural insights

Having an audit as a first step helps to see what is really happening, not what we guess is happening. Evidenced-based clarity is important as we tend to judge ourselves to be less biased **(the bias blindspot)** and higher performing than in reality **(overconfidence bias)**. Even with the best intended managers, frequently a clear pattern is seen of favouring some over others. And a bias blindspot may lead managers to find seemingly 'rational' reasons to always favour the in-group individuals. Left on its own to be corrected by willpower is extremely hard and unlikely to happen. **Confirmation bias** can reinforce our flawed justifications for favouring some over others.

By looking at the entire list of people who are eligible, then we don't use our own private mental list, which is influenced by our own **in-group** of people with whom we feel comfortable. If you rely only on them, then we will miss someone who is capable but not in our circle.

The power of checklists has proven to be effective in reducing errors. They have been hugely influential in the aviation and healthcare sectors. This is because the human mind cannot remember all that it needs to do. The **mental complexity** is too great for slow thinking as the default. Checklists become a structured way to ensure that a process has less influence from mental shortcuts and bias errors. There is untapped potential in using checklists to tackle many of the challenges we face with inequality.

Checklists are also effective in fostering more inclusive collaboration and decision making. For further inspiration, see the design features covered below.

Important design features when creating a checklist

Avoid order bias when creating the checklist

The order of names will have an impact on the rating of the people on the list due to **order bias** and **primacy bias,** which is the tendency to pick one of the first options presented. This usually happens because it's the first choice you read and most likely agree with because subconsciously you may tend to put the people you favour the most (your **in-group**) at the top of the list. **Contrast bias** also plays a role because of the tendency to promote or demote something or someone in a large grouping after a single comparison with one of its peers – typically the previous one in the order. Make sure to randomise the order each person appears in. **Randomise options** in any list you make – including surveys.

On checklists, there are some additional design features that can be incorporated, that while they are not nudges themselves, they do support the overall impact of the checklist as a *Process Design* Inclusion Nudge. Some of these include the following.

Add prompting questions in the beginning

Add questions at the top of the checklist. Seeing and answering these questions as part of the checklist could function as **priming** or **prompting** for more balanced distribution of opportunities. Think of these as similar to speed bumps in the road to slow drivers down. The mental prompters are usually not sufficient alone to change behaviour but they can work in alignment with the purpose of the checklist. Below are some examples.

- → Have I looked at the entire list of people who are eligible to lead this project?
- → Who on the list of people eligible to lead this project, did I not notice?
- → Who on the list of people has been selected before, and how many times?
- → Who else?
- → Who on the list of people could bring something new to this project?

It is important to have several behavioural-based questions and use different ones over time to keep the users reading them.

Frame the questions to have impact

You should test if the checklist will make a bigger difference if you change the wording at the top of the list. Try a framing version on one group and another framing version with another group. You can use several behavioural insights to design the framing, such as these below.

Loss aversion bias

Behavioural insight evidence shows that reversing the sentence to focus on the potential loss, will trigger the loss aversion bias and cause people to look even closer to avoid loss. For example, by asking,

"What will not be achieved, if I don't use all the talents on my team?"

Follow the herd
Evidence shows that we follow the herd and the social norms, that's why it can be impactful to inform others about what the majority is doing and the impact. This can be used as a follow up and to keep momentum. Communicate as part of the checklist what the majority is doing to reinforce new patterns and establish new norms, for example with information such as

"9 out of 10 managers in this organisation have already had better outcomes by using this checklist."

Frame questions to reflect on the patterns revealed
Use **perspective taking** with Flip Questions and lessen confirmation bias, such as with questions like these below.

→ *"If he had longer tenure, would I have given him the assignment?*
→ *"If she was more extrovert, and not so introvert, would I have given her that opportunity?"*

Commitment statement reminder
Intentional statements increase our commitment to action by nearly 50%. There is a bigger impact when we write it down and say it out loud to ourselves and others. So, for even more impact, the manager could write down the commitment statement on the checklist and sign their name to it. Here is an example of a statement of intentionality that could be added to the checklist.

"As an inclusive leader, I want to ensure that all team members have equal and fair opportunities. One step I will do is rotating projects across all eligible people on the team."

This also should be shared with the team and with the manager's manager as that helps to support doing what we say we want to do.

Create sense of being seen when using the checklist
We are primed from infancy to seek out other human faces. We even see faces in objects that don't have faces! Our behaviour is influenced when we feel visible to others. The payment of speeding violation fines is increased

by putting the photo of the driver taken by the radar camera.[117] Seeing our own image creates greater acceptance, ownership, and actually doing the behaviour requested. This also extends to seeing an image of something we value to shift behaviour, such as increased payment of outstanding car taxes by putting a photo of the owner's car on the notice,[118] and increased savings by putting an image of a child on the savings-designated envelope.[119] These visual reminders influence our behaviour towards our intentions, and this can be a powerful way to strengthen the checklist design.

One way to do that is to include a photo of the person using the form (the manager) as part of the form design. Place it next to a personal commitment statement. Even better is if there is a photo of the manager's peer group together holding the checklist. This taps into **collective social norms** of *"this is what my colleagues are doing and this is what I said to them that I would do."*

If the checklist is used with the entire team as the example of Dan, then add pictures of all team members. We feel more accountable to people seen than to names.

Experiment and test the impact

According to the checklist master, **Atul Gawande**, a checklist only becomes good by continuously developing it by testing it in practice and redesigning it together with the people using the checklist.[120] We, therefore, suggest that you **test, reshape, and test again** together with the people using the checklist. Experimenting, testing, following up, and redesigning is an important part of applying behavioural insights designs.

Empower people and groups
instead of disempower

How Diverse Is Your Universe

The Challenge

? Our networks tend to be comprised of people like ourselves. A study found that among White Americans 91% of their network was comprised of White people, among Black Americans 83% of their network was comprised of Black people, and among Latinx Americans 64% of their network was comprised of Latinx people.[121] While the U.S. has a diverse population and *"is on track to be a majority-minority nation by 2044"* (meaning the current minority groups will be in the majority), its neighbourhoods remain racially non-diverse and segregated.[122] Seeing this can be difficult as its your 'normal' and since most around you are like you, it feels comfortable. We miss out on new perspectives, learnings, and innovations when we operate in a group of 'sameness'. Changing this can be a challenge when it's not noticed.

Here is a way to reveal how diverse are the people that you interact with. We first learned about this through a social media posting by **Michelle Silverthorn** 🖐 about an exercise to see how diverse (or not) is your network. She was then the Diversity and Education Director for the Illinois Supreme Court Commission on Professionalism in the U.S. We searched across our network and on the internet, and learned more about this exercise which is often called *"How Diverse is Your Universe?"*. The European-based association called **Intercultural Learning for Pupils and Teachers** 🖐 shares this exercise on their website. Also, **EdChange** 🖐, a U.S.-based organisation focused on building equitable and just communities and organisations, has a variation of this exercise on their website. This exercise is freely and publicly available. **Lisa Kepinski,** Founder of Inclusion Institute, has further developed this to provide more context on how to do it and widen the focus across many contexts that can work in any part of the world.

The Inclusion Nudge

Ask participants "How diverse are the people in your life?". Then, use coloured beads to show aspects of the people they interact with (such using a different coloured bead for each skin colour).

Ask factual questions & a response bead is put in a clear glass to show patterns.

Purpose: Reveal unnoticed patterns of who we connect with, do business with, see, live nearby, and more, and show the gap between self perception and reality. Help people realise the potential loss of diverse experiences and perspectives due to homogeneity in our life.

ATTENTION:
In the write ups that we've seen online, the exercise is typically described in U.S. race/ethnicity context, such as Black, Hispanic, White, Asian, Native American. *You must adjust this within your own context*. This is very important for this exercise to have impact. It must feel relevant to your group and not like a U.S. import. The risk of backfiring is big if you don't customise it. Also, when choosing colours of beads, don't choose yellow for Chinese or red for Native Americans. Avoid what could be stereotyical associations. Use other colours like green, blue, purple.

How To

As a leader you can facilitate this exercise with your team or colleagues.

❶ Design

You may want to use other diversity criteria, such as gender, immigrant, age, abilities, socio-economic status, religion, etc. However, stick with one criteria to reveal the pattern more clearly.

Chose a colour for each aspect of the diversity charateristic.

❷ Materials

Once you have determined your context for what you will be revealing, then you need materials aligned to that.

You need clear (must be see through to have the effect that this design creates) tall containers (such as drinking glasses), one container per each diversity identity option that you've selected for your context. For example, if you were using light skin tone and dark skin tone, each person would have 2 containers. Provide this set of containers to each participant.

You also need coloured beads to represent the people in the categories. An option is to use different coloured beans if beads are not available or above your budget, but if you do this make sure they are all of the same size to have the effect of this exercise.

Each participant gets enough of each of these beads to be able to respond to the questions asked.

❸ Facilitate

Ask each participant to respond (write their answer on a sticky note or piece of paper) to an opening question(s) that indicates their perception about how diverse people are part of their lives. For example, using questions like these,

Do you interact with people who have a different .... than you?
(customise to the diversity that you've selected, such as skin colour, gender, nationality, age, etc.)

If so, what percentage would you say this happens?

Then, introduce that you have a way for them to spot how this happens in their lives. Explain that you will ask a series of questions and each person is to respond by placing the corresponding bead into the designated containers in front of them (each person has their own set of containers per the number of response options). Explain the bead colour chart, and it can be helpful to have this printed out or shown on a slide throughout the exercise.

Ask a range of questions, which may include these. You select questions that fit your context, and you ask based on the diversity identity that you are examining (skin tone/race/ethnicity, gender, age, nationality, etc.).

- My own .... is .... [insert the diversity identity you are using]
- If you have a partner/spouse, their .... is ....
- If you are dating, the last person you dated was ....
- And the current person you are dating is ....
- My best friend's .... is ....
- The person(s) that I sit right next to at work is ....
- My boss is ....
- My boss's boss is ....
- The head of my organisation is ....
- The person who is the receptionist in our organisation is ....
- On the last (or current) work project that I did, the team was predominately ....
- If you attended a professional conference this year, predominately the speakers were .... And the participants were ....
- The last person that you asked for advice, was ....
- My immediate neighbours (right next to where I live) are ....
- If you belong to a hobby or sports club, predominately the people in the club are ....
- Your school teachers were predominately ....
- If you have children, their school teachers are predominately ....
- My doctor is ....
- My dentist is ....
- The person who cuts my hair is ....
- For the last thing that you purchased (coffee, lunch, gas, groceries, clothes, etc.), the person who handled the transaction is ....
- The government head of my city is ....
- The government head of my country is ....
- If you take public transportation, the person you last sat next to is ....
- The author of the last book you read is ....
- The person(s) in the last podcast that you heard was ....
- In my favourite TV program, the main character is ....
- The people in my favourite music group are ....
- If you have followers/contacts on a social media (ex LinkedIn), they are predominately ....
- The most recent 'like' or comment that you posted on social media was for a person who is ....
- If you attend religious services, the people there are predominately ......
- The person that you most admire is ....
- The last person that helped you do something is ....

- The last person that you helped do something is ……..
- The last time you met someone new, that person was ……..
- During the course of a normal day, the people that you predominately come into contact are ……..

You may invite the participants to ask questions for the group to respond to.

❹ Discussion
Invite the participants to look at their containers and reflect on how diverse are the people in their lives. Ask them to compare this to their response to the question asked before starting the exercise.

Is there a gap between your self-perception and what the beads show?
How could this pattern impact you?
(such as their jobs, experiences, leadership, etc.)

How does it impact others?
How does it impact your organisation?
How does it impact the community?
How does it impact society?

Support this 'aha' moment realisation with specific actions (have some ready to offer to start the discussion) that they can do to increase connection with people who are different from them.

In small groups, participants discuss other actions. Share these in plenary.

❺ Commitment & action
Each participant selects one action that they will do, and they write it down on a commitment card. Then, they team up with a learning partner and they take a photo of each other by their containers and holding their action commitment card. They set a specific time when they will follow up with each other to share how did it go. This increases accountability and likelihood of doing the change action.

💻 Online design version
This could be done for an online session by doing it in two parts. First, have participants response to the questions as pre-work, and then they bring their results to the online meeting for discussion. Follow all the How To steps.

Authors' Comments & Behavioural Insights

This is a playful, fun way to realise our hidden patterns of who we interact with. There could be many design variations on this. The purpose of the design is to visibility show how we may not have diversity within our lives and to spark ideas and actions for how we can address this. When you help people see hidden patterns of homogeneity, you empower them to take action, or to be an ally in discussions about privilege or inequality or polarisation or ethnic divides. Many people simply cannot see the issues, and thus believe there are no issues. As a result, they do not engage in the solutions and changes needed. Without empowerment of people and groups we can not achieve equity and inclusion. Helping people realising their hidden patterns is one of the first steps to being an empowering leader. And if you have used this, we are curious to hear about what did you do and how did it go. Drop us an email and we can share with others in the next edition of *The Inclusion Nudges Guidebook* and in other writings.

It seems that this exercise has been around for a while and is cited in several publications but without credit back to the original designer, whom we'd like to give acknowledgement. If you know who first designed this, please let us know. We want to say *'Thank you'*, and learn more about how they have used it.

INCLUSIVE

> **WHAT & HOW**
> I'll make sure to empower people and groups instead of disempower

Bonus Actions!

Tech Free Meetings & Human Connection

It is often underestimated how many barriers for inclusivity are inherent in our unreflected and unproductive ways of working and in our social norms. This intervention and the next intervention called **EMAIL AUTOREPLY RELEASING TIME TO BE PRESENT** both address such challenges.

The Challenge

In most meetings and workshops today, it's a challenge that the participants use technology devices (smart phones, computers, tablets) to write notes, check emails, and for text messages. Researchers have found that technology devices have negative effects on closeness, connection, and conversation quality. Not only when the tech devices are being used, but when present in the room within reaching distance, on the body, or simply visible on the table (even facing down). This limits the brain in having deep conversations.[123]

This is a challenge because benefitting from diversity of knowledge and perspectives in a team and in meetings requires the full attention from all in the group. We need to connect, engage, listen, explore, be curious, and need to combine existing knowledge in new ways to solve tasks and achieve innovation and good decisions.

A part of the challenge is that the brain is addicted to technology devices and it's often an automatic and unreflected behaviour when people reach for the phone and start checking their messages instead of listening to what their colleagues are saying. MIT professor Sherry Turkle has studied the psychology of online connectivity for more than 30 years and addresses this in her book *Reclaiming Conversation: The Power of Talk in a Digital Age*. She argues that we have to seriously rethink how we're integrating technology into our group interactions. We need to be shifting towards being fully present with people around us, not fracturing our attention. She illustrates not only how this is important for our productivity and creativity, but also how technology is undermining human empathy.

It would be easy to tell people not to use these devices at meetings, but the challenges of doing that is that forbidding can foster an even stronger desire to use the device. **Tinna C. Nielsen** started experimenting with ways to apply behavioural insights to have tech free meetings back in 2011, when she worked internally in a global company. She has later refined these interventions through collaboration with teams and groups around the world through her change organisation Move the Elephant for Inclusiveness. Here is how it works.

The Inclusion Nudge

When facilitating group interaction communicate a rule by saying:

"You can call as many breaks as you need to use your tech devices, check emails, messages, take a call.
For now, we all put all our tech devices away, to make sure our full attention is here together. This is out of respect for each other and each other's time. It's also to avoid missing out on your individual knowledge and insights, and to make sure we benefit from the diversity of thought in this group of people.

You should also know that research has proven that technology devices in the room, within reach, visible, on the table or on your body reduces the quality of conversations and your ability to be productive and creative. So, when we have to use our devices today in this meeting, we all do it at the same time.

This means, when you call a break, then you call a break for everyone."

Purpose: Frame the 'call a break for everyone rule' in a way that does not forbid the use of tech devices, but enables people to make a conscious choice when to use it and be considerate about the group. The purpose is also to create an environment in the group characterised by presence and attention.

> **ATTENTION!**
> Do not forbid the use of technology. Forbidding often backfires.

How To

Using this Inclusion Nudge simply requires that you say exactly what is written on the previous page (or as close to as possible).

The framing of this 'rule' is the nudge, and that's why it is absolutely critical that you frame it as described above – each sentence is designed based on behavioural insights. That's why it's important that you read the section Authors' Comments & Behavioural Insights below to learn more about this.

Here is some additional information about how to facilitate this.

For some people this can be a challenge and they might only close their laptop lid halfway or put a piece of paper over it, or put their phone in their pocket. It's important that you follow through and do not begin the meeting or group interaction until all the devices are put away (keep your credibility and integrity).

To address this, call it out and use a bit of humour. For example, say
"If anyone still has their laptop on the table, in their pockets, or within reach, be aware that your tech device still has control over your attention – you don't, so you better put it away. We have time to wait."
Say it with a smile and perhaps add,
"I am just asking based on experience – it's powerful stuff."

Often you will hear people laugh, and see people get up to put it away. Sometimes, people are really creative in how they hide their devices. Call it out and praise them for their 'creativity' and highlight that's what is needed in this meeting. You might also want to call out the amount of effort and energy they spend on not getting separated from their devices – just give them some food for thought.

Maybe you sense a need to facilitate a brief conversation about this and how this influences us in our interactions with each other at work and in relationships. *(Make sure you have read some of the research beforehand. You can find this in the endnotes).*

❗ You might have to reinforce and repeat the 'rule' during meeting – especially after breaks. People easily forget.

💻 Online design version

This Inclusion Nudge applies to not only in-person interactions but also to online meetings and workshops. The tech communications platform is the interaction space for people in the meeting, and that's where their focus is needed. In fact, deep attention is even more needed to make human connection across vast distances with participants who may have different time zones, physical settings, connection quality, and more. Geographically distributed working is becoming a prevailing way that work gets done today. And most people report that they like this approach.[124]

Yet, these types of meetings can also be subject to technology distraction. How often do we hear typing on a keyboard in the background of an online meeting? Or realise that people are not focusing on the discussion because they are multitasking while in the virtual meeting? Our slow, focused mental abilities (system 2) decline significantly when we are multitasking, as shown by research by Daniel Kahneman.[125]

So, in your next online meeting, try out a variation of this design. Use the same approach of *'call a break for everyone'* when participants need to pause the online meeting to check their emails or take a call. Be playful about naming the other tech-distracting behaviours that can occur during virtual meetings, such as online shopping or checking social media. This helps to surface the distracting behaviours that can interfere with the quality of online meetings and it sets a new norm to enable high performance for work interactions done both in-person and in a virtual way. Through this design, we can leverage the advantages of technology to enable online meetings, and at the same time, we can have more purposeful control of the distracting aspects of technology.

Impact

The impact is powerful. It works. Tinna has facilitated this with hundreds of groups across cultures and levels, with young people and executive leaders. It would be natural to think that people would take advantage of this and call a break all the time, but no one does. In many cases where one or two people have called a break they always explain why – *'this simply cannot wait'* meaning that it's important enough to affect the entire group. It is a conscious choice not an automatic unconscious choice. They also often ask to have a break at a specific time to make a short call, meaning that they plan it to have as little effect on the group. This is also a way for them to set themselves free to be fully present.

It would also be natural to think *"I don't have the mandate to do this with people in more powerful positions than myself"*, but trust the research that shows that most people feel that the use of tech devices in group and social interactions harms connection and outcomes, and that all people feel better when the quality of conversation and connection with people is good (not necessarily a recognised need). In all the years, that Tinna has applied this, it has always had a positive effect.

After these sessions and meeting, the majority of times, one or more of the participants have told Tinna how grateful they felt for this 'rule' and many have shared over the years, how this has resulted in more relevant and deep dive conversations, more connection, more empathy, and much more effective meetings and sessions. They apply this themselves when they facilitate meetings. Some also shared how scary it was for them to realise how much the technology devices hijack their attention.

Authors' Comments & Behavioural Insights

Sherry Turkle points to another danger of technology. Online, mostly social media, we learn to fear vulnerability. But vulnerability is exactly what makes us human, productive, empathic, and creative in our personal and professional lives.[126] In life, when we stumble in face-to-face conversation, we reveal ourselves most to each other, and that can be painful. The good thing is that it makes us vulnerable. The dilemma is that we tend to escape such discomfort by turning to our technology devices. In our, Lisa's and Tinna's, view, this is an additional challenge when working in diverse groups that are making an effort to leverage their diversity to solve a task. Because as research[127] shows, it is hard to apply diversity and it can feel uncomfortable because it will require that we explore, question, do something new, and have conversations we have not had before. All of this is about vulnerability. So, what if members of a work group unconsciously turn to their tech devices to avoid feelings of discomfort and vulnerability fostered by effort in the group to leverage diversity? If that's the case, then we do not get access to diversity of thinking and do not benefit from this. Then, all the effort of composing diverse teams, mitigating bias, and building inclusive capabilities is wasted due to the use and presence of technology devices in meetings and group interactions. What a shame and what a waste! That only makes it more compelling to apply this 'rule' and lead inclusively.

Why it works: behavioural insights

This designed intervention works because it sets the participants free from the culture of always being available, it **sets the mind free** to be present, and it does **not prohibit** them from using their devices. It sets them free from the mental hijacking and addiction of their phone, free to call a break when they need it, free to listen and be present instead of sharing their attention between people and devices. Being guided in the right direction and having the **freedom to opt out** is the very essence of nudging.

It is a well-known psychological mechanism that people don't like it when others forbid them to do something that they want to do. It's also well known that we like to feel empowered to make choices and have control of our own lives and current situations. Our **social orientation** is also a strong behavioural influencer. It matters to most to human beings (except psychopaths!) to be accepted by their peers and to **belong to an in-group**. This makes us adjust our behaviour to fit the **norm** (this 'rule' is calling out a new norm). We don't want to be outliers and don't want to burden the group.

It works because you appeal to the participants' **tribal mentality** and natural social orientation, as well as the feeling of **belonging to a group**. It appeals to their **identity**, *'I am the kind of person that respects others.'* And we don't like to burden our group by asking for breaks. We also burden the group when checking emails and not being present during a meeting but we don't feel it like that. However, we do feel it when we have to ask for a break to not be present. This intervention also triggers the **loss aversion bias** where we are more motivated by what we may lose than by what we may gain.

Bonus Actions!

Email Autoreply Releasing Time to Be Present

The Challenge

? An often-overlooked barrier to inclusiveness is cognitive overload and time pressure. This hinders us from being present and thinking reflectively about our interactions with people and ways of working. We are in the midst of a technological revolution. The World Economic Forum, and many other organisations, have identified critical skills needed in the future, which include the ability to think critically and creatively. These skills are under pressure when we experience cognitive overload and time pressure. One of the cognitive mechanisms to cope with this complexity and overload is mental shortcuts (biases). These are a key barrier to being inclusive.

We know from research[128] that one of the major time-stealing activities that most people engage in is email and social media. When we stop working on a task to check emails it takes the brain about 23 minutes to get back into deep task-solving mode. Part of the problem is that many people allow emails to control their time and day when it should be the opposite. Part of the reason is the perception that we have to answer emails as quick as possible, making us check emails regularly during the day.

What if we changed this perception by setting up the email system to reframe our own perception and that of others? And we do that in a way that releases time and energy to be present, reflect, deep dive into tasks, and set our mind free to think critically and creatively? Here is how **Tinna C. Nielsen** does this in Move the Elephant for Inclusiveness, based on inspiration from the Founder of Women Reignite, **Soulaima Gourani** 🧠.

The Inclusion Nudge

Set your e-mail autoreply to always be on.
Write a message that you only check emails a couple of days a week (or at a specific time during the day).

See below **Tinna C. Nielsen's** example.

Thank you for reaching out to me.
I only check and reply to emails a couple of times a week.
Why? I become very ineffective and less creative when having to check emails throughout the day. Research shows it take 23 minutes for our brain to get back into a task after checking emails/social media. That doesn't make sense!
I am working on designing innovative ways to create inclusive organisations, communities, and societies worldwide – I do that in collaboration with others and that requires my full attention.
So, thank you for your patience.
You will hear from me within a week.
If you deem it to be REALLY important and just can't wait, please send me a text message: [telephone number] (expect delay in response due to travelling).
I'll be looking forward to connecting with you.

Kind regards,
Tinna C. Nielsen

Purpose: Set yourself free, create time to do your best work, increase patience in others, and create a new norm by a designing a way to tackle some of the key conditions where bias arises (fatigue, mental overload, and complexity).

How To

Set your e-mail autoreply to always be on. Write a message that you only check emails a certain day a week or time a day. In framing this message, it's important to design it based on behavioural insights for it to be effective. So, be sure to share,

→ something personal about your passion
→ something about releasing the time to be innovative
→ the research about the negative impact of checking emails often.

By doing this you will help people reflect: *"Is it really important that I send this message?"* You will also set people free as they can get in touch with you in another way. And you will trigger patience. It is equally important to give people the option to get in touch with you in other ways in case they cannot wait.

Of course, it's important to design this in accordance with the job you have. For Tinna who submitted this example, as a knowledge worker, self-employed, and social entrepreneur, she does not need to answer emails immediately. But she does check the email inbox most days to look for emails from people she is collaborating with and when she knows there is a deadline.

Many versions have been made of this autoreply. Some write that they check-in during the morning, others in the afternoon (do it when your energy is low, and spend you higher energy on people around you and work that requires your critical and creative thinking), some only check on Fridays, others only on Mondays. Make your version that fits your energy, job, work, and life. Remember to share with us how you do it and how it works for you.

Impact

Tinna made her autoreply in 2016 after reading about the research showing the negative impact of emails and social media on our work and social relations. After time tracking her own work for a while, Tinna realised that she too allowed email to eat up most of her work day (up to 70 %), making her ineffective and drained of energy. This made her feel, that she was not being true to herself and what she stands for. This reply states a message about that to herself and to other people.

When Tinna tells about this autoreply, the most common reaction from people is *"... that is not possible for me"* or *"... you must lose a lot of jobs that way ..."* or *"wow ... you must be getting a lot of text messages from people deeming it important that you answer immediately ..."*.

But the fact is that in all these years, Tinna has received only 18 text messages from people asking her to reply quickly (and 6 of those where from the same person within the same week). She has lost one job from someone who did not write her a text message to react quickly, and she has received feedback from 54 people that they love her autoreply. And she has freed up a lot of time to create and be present and re-gained her passion for the work she does. Plus, she can now do the emailing in half the time that she used to spend on this.

It has changed her perception of having to be available all the time to others (a negative consequence of technology, social media, etc.) and it has changed the expectation of other people of having access to other people all the time – and perhaps more importantly, it has made them reflect on what they send to others in an email and what's important.

Authors' Comments & Behavioural Insights

Why it works: behavioural insights

This intervention does not directly nudge people to be inclusive. We consider this an important enabler to create ways of working that free up the human mind to be able to be present by **reducing cognitive overload** and mental shortcuts (bias). The more time pressured we are, the more biased we are in our judgements and decision-making. And bias is one of the biggest barriers to achieving inclusion. As complexity continues to grow in our lives, we will depend increasingly on our mental shortcuts to handle all of this stimuli. We need to broaden our scope for coming up with solutions for how to mitigate bias in how we operate by actually *changing how we operate*. So, indirectly this intervention supports inclusiveness and that why we share it.

Several behavioural insights are applied in this design and you can use these to address many other challenges.

Giving a reason triggers collaboration
When you have a request of people, it's important to give a reason – the irrational aspect is, that it doesn't matter what is the reason. It's the *'because'* and *'why'* that trigger the automatic collaborative instinct. This is demonstrated in an experiment by social psychologist Ellen Langer. People waiting in line to use a copy machine were asked by a person in the line *"Excuse me, I have five pages. May I use the copying machine?"*, and 60 % agreed to let the person skip the line. But surprisingly, when asked *"Excuse me, I have five pages. May I use the copying machine because I have to make some copies?"* – 93 % agreed to let the person get in front of the line. The researcher also tested other 'reasons' but it was not the reason itself that made people collaborate, but the reason that they got a reason.[129]

Giving a time frame triggers patience
A body of research has proven that giving people a time for how long they have to wait increases their patience. A well-known example is the traffic light countdown timer, showing pedestrians how long they have to wait at the red light which reduces dangerous jaywalking.[130]

Giving an option to act triggers autonomy
Autonomy is people's need to perceive that they have choices, that what they are doing is of their own volition, and that they are the source of their own actions. The way information and situations are framed either promotes the likelihood that a person will perceive autonomy or undermines it. And this has a critical impact on how we behave and the actions we take. In the email autoreply, giving people the option to judge if their message is important and to reach out via phone and text messaging, gives the feeling of autonomy, and reduces the need for an immediate reply.

These behavioural insights can be used in many settings. We really need to start thinking more broadly about how to foster more inclusive cultures, environments, behaviour, and mindsets by looking at the root causes of why and when bias arises.

Publicly Available Resources

See other ideas in this article, *"6 Ways to Set Boundaries Around Email"* by Sarah K. Peck[131] who calls out that *"we must get better at saying no"* or risk being drowned by email and messaging.

Bonus Actions!

Simplify Accountability for Achieving Commitments & Goals

The Challenge

There can be a lot of positive statements and wishes when talking about inclusion, equity, and diversity. Often it is assumed that this will bring about changes in behaviour, culture, and collaboration, but this is rarely the case. While goal setting and accountability is often an organisational value and an expected leadership competency, this is usually not designed in a way that enables the shift towards the desired outcomes. Status quo preference thinking and other biases can work against making change happen. The result is that trust and commitment are questioned when achievement of goals is not seen by others. Ineffectiveness, frustration, and lack of credibility can become the unintended outcome. There are better ways to make change for inclusiveness happen rather than relying upon willpower alone.

The Inclusion Nudge

Integrate in organisational processes personal commitments and accountability based on behavioural insights:
Decide, Write, Tell, Show, Share

Purpose: Close the gap between 'intentions and doing' by implementing enablers for follow through on goals and commitments.

How To

These seemingly simple steps can have a big impact on achieving our goals for behavioural change. **Lisa Kepinski,** Founder of Inclusion Institute, and **Tinna C. Nielsen,** Founder of Move the Elephant for Inclusiveness, have experimented with these simple behavioural interventions and with thousands of people in organisations around the world. This is how the most impactful version has been designed.

→ **Decide** on one small action (reduces complexity) that addresses the most common trigger of the behaviour you want to change. **Plan** what and how to do it.
→ **Write** it down. Do this in your own handwriting (improves memory), not typing on a device, and **sign your name** (makes your commitment salient).
→ **Tell** your commitment to yourself by saying it out loud. Make a **memory recall** to this commitment, like a title. **Tell colleagues** about what you are going to do.
→ **Show** it to a colleague. Have a colleague take a photo of you and your written commitment and send it to you.
→ **Share** with a colleague. **Meet up** on a regular basis to **share** what you have done and what you learned. Schedule time. **Celebrate** improvements together.

Online design version

These inclusive commitment nudges can be used in both in-person and virtual meetings. When using in virtual meetings, you can have all participants write their individual commitments in the online communication platform's chat function or on a shared whiteboard that all can view. Also, next time you have a virtual meeting, begin the meeting with a 'commitment check-in' where every participant writes and shares what they have done and how it worked out. This is a great way to capture individual learning and turn it into wider organisational learning.

Impact

We have used this approach in numerous team development workshops and leadership programmes, design sessions, and co-creation processes that we've led on creating behaviour and system change to make inclusion the default and the norm. We have seen stronger levels of sticking with the statements of intentions for change, and heard back from many that the process has worked well for them to achieve their set goals.

Authors' Comments & Behavioural Insights

This kind of accountability should be applied everywhere we need ourselves and other people to make commitments and achieve goals. Too many of us can say all the right things, but we don't really change behaviour and are never held accountable. This ought to become the default and norm everywhere we want to make change and improvements.

Why it works: behavioural insights
Decide on small action
It's important to reduce complexity. Many options, even good ones, and many good intentions can cause **decision paralysis** that makes us retreat to default behaviour and plans.[132]

Plan critical steps
Research shows that self-control and willpower are not enough to help us achieve our goals because it is an exhaustible resource.[133] Making a plan as simple as reflecting on teh exact date, time, and how to do it, makes it more likely that we will do it.[134]

Writing in hand
Professor Gail Matthews from Dominican University of California has studied goal setting and achieving goals extensively. Her research has found that 42 % of people in the workplace are more likely to achieve their goals by writing them down.

Tell & show
Public commitment and cues of being watched influence our behaviour and increases or ethics.[135]

Share & follow up
Additionally, 70 % of people are more likely to achieve their goals when sending weekly updates to peers as compared to only 35 % who didn't share.[136]

The prospect of a follow-up activates feelings of accountability.[137] The best results involved commitment to action, accountability to peers, and regular updates.[138]

Most people report that having a learning buddy to support and be supported by has the biggest impact. It makes a difference that someone cares and that it matters what they do and don't do. Turns out that people like to be held accountable – so let's do it some more.

> These last three examples give you as a leader and as someone who wants to have a better balance in how you work, live, operate, connect with others, and thrive, some very tangible actions you can do immediately. All of which can help you lead more inclusively.

> We wish you all the best in your everyday experimentation with all 30 Inclusion Nudges in this Action Guide.

Watch these TEDx talks for more inspiration

To experience the power of Inclusion Nudges, we recommend that you watch our TEDx talks where we illustrate how these work.

TEDx Talk: Outsmarting Our Brains to Mitigate Bias in Talent Decisions
https://www.youtube.com / watch?v=4DpZm0GNqfQ

Hear how Lisa Kepinski addressed resistance from executives to increasing women in senior leadership. An interactive Inclusion Nudge helped them see the hidden patterns of unintentional exclusion and unequal opportunities. They moved from resistance to ownership, co-creation, and action-taking, resulting in several promotions of women in the next 6 months.

TEDx Talk: Nudge Behaviour for a More Inclusive World
https://www.youtube.com / watch?v=VggAqa0xOwM

Take part in the interactive experiment that Tinna C. Nielsen is doing in the beginning of this talk. This is an example of a motivational Inclusion Nudge making people feel the need to change how they make judgements and decisions. The result is people taking active part in combating inequality by changing behaviours, cultures, and systems in their sphere of influence.

It's time to lead inclusively.
Let's make inclusion the norm everywhere, for everyone.
You make it happen!

SECTION 4

How You Take This Forward

> LEADERS stand out by how they take action for diversity, equity, and inclusion

Leading inclusively is needed in times of extreme change

The global world is changing at a pace and scale never experienced before. At the time of writing this *Action Guide for Leaders* in June 2020, we are in the midst of a global crisis of health, social, and economic dimension. Going forward, this will most certainly have lasting impact changing our world, including the way we work, connect, and live.

> What kind of leadership will this require?
>
> What kind of leaders will people trust and follow?
>
> What kind of leader do you want to be?

Unprecedented changes have been a part of our lives for much longer than this current situation due to technological transformations, demographic changes in the make-up of our workforces and societies, environmental catastrophes, economic turmoil, and much more. As human beings, we are hardwired for coping with change and hardship. But all of these changes still put a toll on our mental capacity, our ability to navigate complexity, and also collaborate across identity and knowledge diversity. We must be capable of interacting, innovating, and making decisions in an increasingly complex environment.

> When faced with challenges, are you leading in a way that is encompassing all the people around you?
>
> What kind of standard do you set for others when they see how you work?
>
> How do you empower people to engage with each other and seek out a wide range of ideas as part of their daily work?

The era we are currently living in, called the Fourth Industrial Revolution, is characterised by technology, artificial intelligence, robotics, and machine learning. This brings fundamental changes in our lives, organisations, and societies, and it is also questioning our value as human beings – *'what can humans do that technology can't do better and faster?'*. Reports from international intergovernmental organisations, the World Economic Forum, and researchers have repeatedly given calls to action for leaders to develop organisations and societies that strengthen the capacity to leverage the human potential of creativity, empathy, exploration, and critical thinking. For organisations and societies to remain agile and innovative, we need to make sure we unlock these human attributes, and that we all play a part in leveraging all the diversity of experiences, perspectives, and knowledge that are available in our organisations, teams, schools, cities, communities, and society.

How will you respond to this call to action?

How will you make sure to be inclusive
of the multiple resources of people?

This is about much more than leveraging the full potential of people to perform and innovate well. This is about the well-being and health of the billions of people living in our communities and working in our organisations. It's also the only way to reverse the damaging path we have been on for too long where increasing inequality, racism, declining social mobility, and polarisation have increased with damaging results.

{ Leaders, each in our organisations and communities, and collectively around the globe, play a vital role in reaching the needed new solutions to create a socially, culturally, environmentally, and economically sustainable world. Maintaining the status quo is not an option for meeting the future. }

There is no 'business as usual' and no space for 'this is what we normally do'. All people need to be involved in making the necessary changes happen (whatever these are), and inclusive collaboration, inclusive idea generation, and inclusive decision making are the way forward.

When we develop and design, and when we make changes, regardless of being small or big, we must be deliberate about being inclusive by applying a lens of diversity, equality, and inclusion.

→ How will you be an inclusive leader in everything you do to support this moving forward?

The Director of the London School of Economics and Political Science, Minouche Shafik, has said

> "In the past jobs were about muscles, now they're about brains, but in future they'll be about the heart." [139]

This is also the case for inclusive leadership. And this will require courage.

The original definition of **'courage'** is from the Latin word *cor*, which means heart and the original meaning was *'to speak one's mind by telling all one's heart'*. This can be interpreted in many ways, but the great leaders we have met are inclusive, and they have the courage to let go of who they think they are supposed to be and show up as they are. They are willing to be vulnerable, meaning to do something where there are no guarantees, and do things that they cannot control and predict. And maybe most importantly, they engage in situations and conversations that can be uncomfortable. They just embrace it because they can practice self-compassion when they fall short, as well as offer empathy and compassion towards others. It turns out that courage and vulnerability are a foundation for inclusivity, and also the birthplace of innovation, creativity, belonging, joy, and empowerment.[140]

{ Courageous leaders strive to practice inclusivity and change the excluding patterns in our organisations, communities, and society. }

With Inclusion Nudges you can make this happen without having to feel it as extra work, and instead make it a natural and integrated part of your daily and strategic leadership.

How you make it happen

You can easily make inclusion the norm by applying the inclusive actions described in this Action Guide and using a process cycle of everyday experimentation to guide you.

All steps in this process are needed; don't overlook any of them. This will ensure your commitment to action, your credibility that you do what you say you want to do, and your ability to be a more effective inclusive leader with impact.

Call upon your courage and go forward. You make it happen!

What and how I'll do this

LEADING INCLUSIVELY
How you do everyday experimentations – step by step

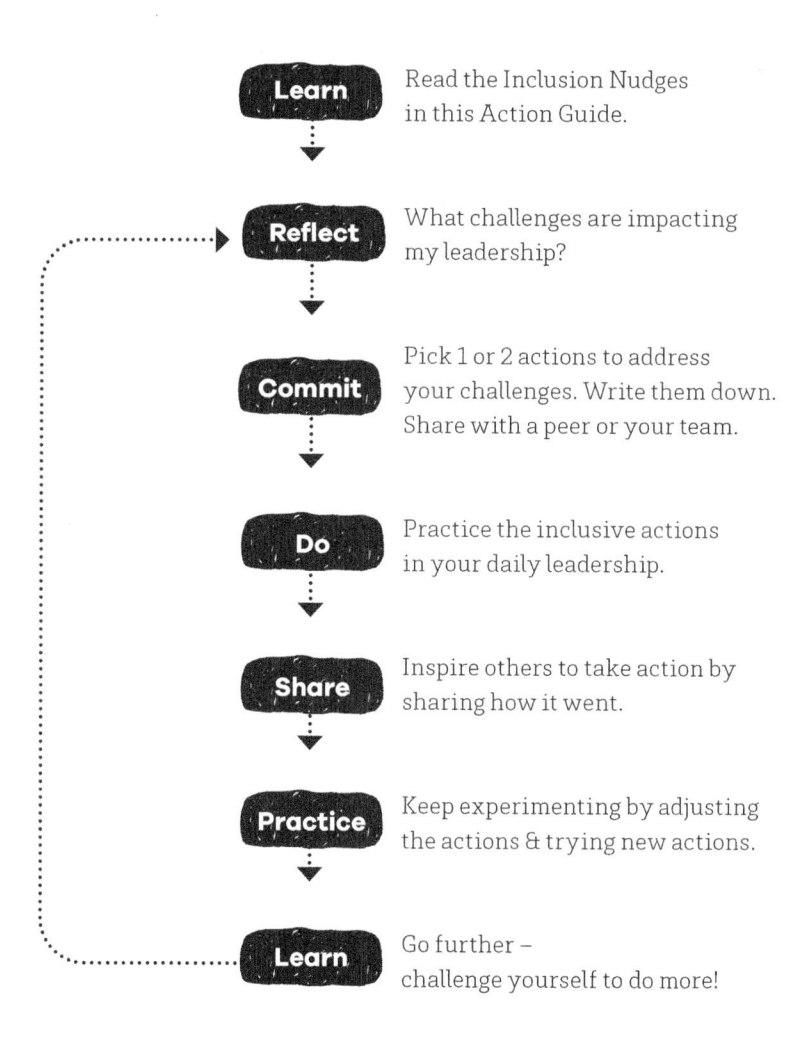

Learn — Read the Inclusion Nudges in this Action Guide.

Reflect — What challenges are impacting my leadership?

Commit — Pick 1 or 2 actions to address your challenges. Write them down. Share with a peer or your team.

Do — Practice the inclusive actions in your daily leadership.

Share — Inspire others to take action by sharing how it went.

Practice — Keep experimenting by adjusting the actions & trying new actions.

Learn — Go further – challenge yourself to do more!

There are many ways to keep learning and move forward.
See the resources on the Inclusion Nudges resource platform
www.inclusion-nudges.org

Get more Inclusion Nudge designs in the other books in this
ACTION GUIDE SERIES

INCLUSION NUDGES FOR TALENT SELECTION
Action Guide with 30 examples

WHAT Practical way to de-bias processes to recruit and promote people, staff great teams, and enhance the diversity of talents of all people by applying Inclusion Nudges and making inclusion the norm.

WHO For you who are involved in selecting people for jobs and composing diverse teams or in any other way involved in talent selection processes in your organisation or community.

INCLUSION NUDGES FOR MOTIVATING ALLIES
Action Guide with 30 examples

WHAT Practical ways to show people issues of inequality, discrimination and unconscious bias that they are blind to, and to feel the need to engage in the change. As a result, they will automatically be allies.

WHO For you who are a leader, diversity, equity, and inclusion professional, human resource professional, social activist, human rights advocate, or member in an employee or citizen network or group. You want to motivate more people to get engaged in making changes in organisations and communities.

Order your paperbacks or e-books now:
www.inclusion-nudges.org

THE INCLUSION NUDGES GUIDEBOOK

FOR CHANGE MAKERS – 100 Inclusion Nudges

WHAT For you who are a change maker, leader, developer, social activist, or innovator leading change. You work on organisational or societal development, diversity, equity, inclusion, social impact, human resources, human rights, the UN Global Goal, and/or other areas of change for greater inclusivity. You want practical designs and inspiration to make impact. *The Inclusion Nudges Guidebook* is your comprehensive go-to resource to make inclusion happen with over 100 actions that you can do.

WHO For you who want to make changes for social impact, inclusion, diversity, gender parity, and equality, who work in human resources, are a diversity, equity, and inclusion professional, and in any other way leading change.

Order your paperback now:
www.inclusion-nudges.org

Moving forward as a global community

From around the world, tens of thousands of leaders, project managers, change makers, human resource and diversity & inclusion professionals like you, are exploring how they can apply the Inclusion Nudges change approach in their processes of selecting talent and building diverse teams. This strengthens people, organisations, and communities by reducing the influence of bias and increases inclusivity. Their feedback has been overwhelmingly positive. Appreciation has been expressed for the impact and the evidence-based grounding in behavioural science as well as the real-life expertise of making inclusion, diversity, equity, and belonging a reality and the norm.

This Action Guide is a result of people sharing their experiences with applying Inclusion Nudge actions, including their own design variations, and the results. The *Action Guide for Talent Selection* is part of the Inclusion Nudges global initiative, with the purpose to leverage diverse human talents and potential, and creating more inclusive behaviour, culture, processes, and systems. We do this by applying behavioural insights and making inclusion the norm everywhere, for everyone.

Together, we can create a profound transformation in organisational and societal development to achieve more inclusive and sustainable development. You make it actionable.

All action matters, both in our own 'local' context and collectively in a 'global' context. We need to inspire and empower each other to make it happen. That's why reciprocal sharing of practical actions proven to work is important. It is why we founded this movement. We would be grateful to hear from you how you put the Inclusion Nudges in the Action Guide into action. Share how it works out.

Send us an email: contact@inclusion-nudges.org

Thank you, *Lisa & Tinna*

Lisa Kepinski & Tinna C. Nielsen

Founders of the Inclusion Nudges Global Initiative, Authors of *The Inclusion Nudges Guidebook* (2020) and *Inclusion Nudges Action Guide Series*

It's time to lead inclusively.
Let's make inclusion the norm everywhere, for everyone.
You make it happen!

Getting Clear on the Principles

The Inclusion Nudges initiative principles

The global Inclusion Nudges change initiative is building on a very simple idea. When we (people who want to make changes) design interventions that nudge the unconscious mind to be inclusive by default, then Tinna and Lisa write exactly what and how it was done to make it work. Then, we share it with others who can then do it in their context. From this, we developed the global initiative for others to do the same. Here are some of the Inclusion Nudges global movement principles.

Sharing
This initiative is based on collaboration, co-creation, and sharing to enable other change makers. Sharing what has worked for you is needed to keep this movement progressing. What you share inspires others and sparks global change to make inclusion the default and the norm. Without sharing, there is no initiative. Your insights and experiences are needed. Your colleagues in the global community are counting on you to do this.

Reciprocity
You can make social change happen. Taking (benefiting) and sharing (giving to others) are important to enable as many people as possible to make inclusion the norm. You can do this by joining forces, exchanging knowledge, offering examples, and doing both 'give & get' and gift giving for the greater good. These are all vital ways to keep this movement going. And you are at the centre of this.

Open source
The Inclusion Nudges initiative is for everybody. It is for those who want to use the examples being shared, those who design without applying, and those doing both. And it is for those who are curious and want to learn more. We all need ideas for what can work, and to be able to freely access this. This is why we didn't copyright the concept or approach. Knowledge shouldn't be hoarded to one's self or for sale to a select few, but shared with all in the world. That is how social change can happen.

Though we have coined the term 'Inclusion Nudge' and developed the framework of the three types of Inclusion Nudges, we have not copyrighted or trademarked these concepts because we believe in sharing, open source, and professional trust.

> In support of this approach, we have applied the Creative Commons Attribution-Non-Commercial-Share Alike 4.0 International license[141] to the Inclusion Nudges concept.
>
> ![CC BY-NC-SA]
>
> Note that our writing in *The Inclusion Nudges Guidebook,* the Inclusion Nudges Action Guide Series books, and the Inclusion Nudges blog articles are under copyright permission.
>
> Citation: *"From Inclusion Nudges Action Guide Series © 2020 Tinna C. Nielsen and Lisa Kepinski. All rights reserved."*

Take a quick look at the next two pages for more information on how to apply the principles in practice.

What's okay & what's NOT okay

Based on our experiences over the past couple of years as our Inclusion Nudges change methodology and the examples in the guidebook have spread globally, and the term Inclusion Nudges has grown in popularity, **we realise there is a growing need to clarify what sharing, reciprocity, and open source means. Some people seem to have misunderstood. So, here is what's okay and not okay.**[142]

Thank you for honouring
the Inclusion Nudges initiative principles.

It's **okay** to use the Inclusion Nudge examples of your peers	It's **not okay** to use the examples and pretend it's your own design

Tell who designed it and where you got it from!

It's **okay** to experiment with the design of the Inclusion Nudge examples	It's **not okay** to keep the learning and outcome to yourself

Share with us how it worked for you!

It's **okay** to write about Inclusion Nudges in your own books and articles	It's **not okay** if you don't mention that you didn't come up with the concept

Tell people about the original source!

It's **okay** to use the examples to make change in your sphere of influence	It's **not okay** to use it for your own or your organisation's commercial use

Direct people to *The Inclusion Nudges Guidebook* to get the examples!

It's **okay** to tell your clients about Inclusion Nudges and give examples	It's **not okay** that you set up your consultancy based on the Inclusion Nudges concept

Use it in your work, but don't sell it like you created the concept!

It's **okay** to inform others about Inclusion Nudges	It's **not okay** that you keep it to yourself when you benefit from this

Tell others about the free resources on the website, so they benefit too!

| It's **okay** to share in your network about Inclusion Nudges | It's **not okay** to share so you can sell it tied to a membership fee to your organisation |

Tell all about the resources, but don't sell it or limit it to just a few!

| It's **okay** that you tell about Inclusion Nudges in your presentations | It's **not okay** that you copy presentations designed & given by Lisa and Tinna |

Make your own by being inspired – and reference the source!

| It's **okay** that you see a need for the guidebook in other languages | It's **not okay** that you translate it without the authors' permission |

Reach out to us to discuss opportunities for this!

| It's **okay** to share about Inclusion Nudges on your organisation's platform | It's **not okay** to copy and paste direct text from the guidebook |

Put the Inclusion Nudges website link on your platform!

| It's **okay** to create a conference on Inclusion Nudges | It's **not okay** to do this without informing or involving Lisa and Tinna |

Engage us to represent accurately the Inclusion Nudges methodology!

| It's **okay** to be inspired and share the guidebook in your organisation | It's **not okay** to copy the guidebook and pass that around |

Buy multiple copies of the guidebook and give as gifts to your colleagues!

REFERENCE SECTION

About the Authors

Endnotes

"Never doubt that a small group
of thoughtful, committed citizens
can change the world;
indeed, it's the only thing that ever has."

Margaret Mead,
Anthropologist, 1901–1978

About the authors

Founders of the INCLUSION NUDGES global initiative

Tinna C. Nielsen

Founder
Move the Elephant
for Inclusiveness

Lisa Kepinski

Founder
Inclusion Institute

Lisa Kepinski and Tinna C. Nielsen co-authored *The Inclusion Nudges Guidebook* and co-founded the Inclusion Nudges global initiative in 2013. For this innovative work, Lisa and Tinna were named to The Economist's & The Telegraph's Global Diversity List "Top 10 List" in 2015, 2016, & 2017. Also, the Inclusion Nudges Initiative was shortlisted for a European Diversity Award in 2019. We also write for the World Economic Forum's blog Agenda.

{ To learn more or have a discussion, please contact us at contact@inclusion-nudges.org }

Tinna C. Nielsen

Move the Elephant for Inclusiveness
tinna@movetheelephant.org

Tinna is an anthropologist, social entrepreneur, and behavioural designer pioneering innovative approaches for practitioners and change makers to accelerate inclusiveness, diversity, gender parity, and equality as a means to achieve better innovation, collaboration, and sustainable development for all people in our organisations, communities, cities, and societies.

For the past 19 years Tinna has specialised in applying insights from behavioural and social sciences to design impactful solutions, and change behaviours, cultures, and systems to be inclusive by default and as the norm. In 2013, Tinna founded the change-organisation Move the Elephant for Inclusiveness, partnering with private and public organisations, NGOs, and governments worldwide, as well as collaborating with people at all levels of society and in all sectors. Tinna is also a strategic partner for inclusiveness and gender parity at the United Nations, as well as educating UN leaders and gender focal points. Tinna has extensive experience in inclusive leadership development at all levels and in all functions, and she is internationally recognised for her interactive style of influencing, teaching, facilitating, co-designing, and giving talks (TEDx talk in 2017). In addition to writing *The Inclusion Nudges Guidebook*, Tinna has co-authored social innovation books about how to redesign social welfare systems and do inclusive community co-creation based on behavioural insights.

The World Economic Forum (WEF) honoured Tinna as a Young Global Leader (YGL) in 2015. She is taking part in the YGL community to create solutions to improve the state of the world. She served as co-chair of the WEF Global Future Council on Behavioural Sciences 2016-18, and is part of the WEF Expert Network, and a regular writer for the WEF blog Agenda. Tinna is Fellow at the RSA, Royal Society of Arts, and serves on several advisory boards. Tinna is volunteering support to social innovation initiatives where she lives and worldwide.

Tinna is now living in Denmark with her three daughters and husband.

Lisa Kepinski

Inclusion Institute
lisa.kepinski@inclusion-institute.com

Lisa partners with organisations on how to successfully achieve their goals for creating a more inclusive culture for sustainable growth. Her deep expertise in organisational development and behavioural science integrated with inclusive culture make her a unique resource. With nearly 20 years' experience as a global inclusion & diversity executive for AXA, Microsoft, & HP, Lisa knows well the realities of creating change inside large, global organisations. With deep experience as an internal inclusion change leader, Lisa founded in 2013 the Inclusion Institute and focuses on designing organisational and behavioural change strategy and actions to increase inclusion, equity, and diversity. She also coaches change makers and leaders to enable them to carry this work forward in their organisations. Lisa's clients are from a wide range of sectors including multinationals, businesses, NGOs, governments, universities, and directly with change makers.

As an inclusion and behavioural change thought leader, Lisa frequently speaks at conferences, offers webcasts, and advises organisations. In June 2017, Lisa gave a TEDx talk on the need to design for inclusive behavioural change. She conducts research and writes to help further the practice of inclusion, equity, and diversity. She does this always with a practical application focus. In addition to *The Inclusion Nudges Guidebook*, she has co-conducted global studies on improving the effectiveness of women networks, inclusion & diversity actions with impact (published by Newsweek), and most recently on inclusive remote work. Lisa works with groups to encourage their focus on inclusion, such as by serving on several advisory boards, chairing conferences, founding the Europe-based Global D&I Forum, and as an expert panellist for Global Diversity & Inclusion Benchmarks.

Lisa has lived in 5 countries and travelled extensively in her global roles. She was born and educated in the US (with degrees in social psychology and socio-linguistics), has worked in Europe for over 20 years, has 2 adult daughters, and lives in Germany with her husband.

Endnotes

1   **ARTICLE ON INCLUSION NUDGES.** Ellen McGirt, Fortune's RaceAhead: Culture and Diversity in Corporate America, 9 May 2019

2   **GROUPTHINK.** Irving L. Janis, 1972

3   **MAXIMIZING THE GAINS AND MINIMIZING THE PAINS OF DIVERSITY: A POLICY PERSPECTIVE.** Adam D. Galinsky, Andrew R. Todd, Astrid C. Homan, Katherine W. Phillips, Evan P. Apfelbaum, Stacey J. Sasaki, Jennifer A. Richeson, Jennifer B. Olayon, & William W. Maddux, Perspectives on Psychological Science, vol 10, no 6, pgs 742-748, 2015

4   **THE DIFFERENCE: HOW DIVERSITY CREATS BETTER GROUPS, FIRMS, SCHOOLS AND SOCIETIES.** Scott E. Page, 2007; **DIVERSITY MATTERS.** Vivian Hunt, Dennis Layton, & Sara Prince, McKinsey & Company, 2 February 2015; **MAKING GREAT DECISIONS.** C. Heath & O. Sibony, McKinsey Quarterly, April 2013

5   **THE BUSINESS CASE FOR DIVERSITY IN THE WORKPLACE IS NOW OVERWHELMING.** Vijay Eswaran, World Economic Forum Agenda, 29 April 2019; **DELIVERING THROUGH DIVERSITY.** Vivian Hunt, Sara Prince, Sundiatu Dixon-Fyle, & Lareina Yee, McKinsey & Company, January 2018; **WHY DIVERSITY AND INCLUSION MATTER: QUICK TAKE.** Catalyst, 1 August 2018; **INNOVATION, DIVERSITY AND MARKET GROWTH.** Syliva Ann Hewlett, Melinda Marshall, Laura Sherbin, & Tara Gonsalves, Center for Talent Innovation, September 2013; **CREATING A CULTURE WHERE EMPLOYEES SPEAK UP.** Sylvia Ann Hewlett, Harvard Business Review, 8 January 2016; **DIVERSITY WINS: HOW INCLUSION MATTERS.** Sundiatu Dixon-Fyle, Kevin Dolan, Vivian Hunt, & Sara Prince, McKinsey, 19 May 2020

6   **A PEER PRESSURE EXPERIMENT: RECREATIONS OF THE ASCH CONFORMITY EXPERIMENT WITH ROBOTS.** Jurgen Brandsetter, Peter Racz, Eduard Clay Beckner, & Benitz Sandoval, IEEE/RSJ International Conference on Intelligent Robots and Systems, 14-18 September 2014; **NO NEED TO FAKE IT: REPRODUCTION OF THE ASCH EXPERIMENT WITHOUT CONFERATES.** K. Mori & M Arai, International Journal of Psychology, 1 October 2010

7   **THE 4 STATGES OF PSYCHOLOGY SAFETY: DEFINING THE PATH TO INCLUSION AND INNOVATION.** Timothy R. Clark, 2020

8   **PSYCHOLOGY CONDITIONS OF PERSONAL ENGAGEMENT AND DISENGAGEMENT AT WORK.** William A. Kahn, Academy of Management Journal, vol 33, no 4, pgs 692-724, 1990

9   **PSYCHOLOGY SAFTEY AND LEARNING BEHAVIOUR IN WORK TEAMS.** Amu Edmondson, Administrative Science Quarterly, vol 44, no 2, pgs 350-383, 1999

10 **A SHORT NOTE ON ACCENT-BIAS, SOCIAL IDENTITY AND ETHNOCENTRISM.** Rahul Chakraborty, Advances in Language and Literary Studies, vol 8, no 4, 31 August 2017; **THE DETECTION OF FRENCH ACCENT BY AMERICAN LISTENERS.** James Emil Flege, Journal of Acoustical Society of America, vol 76, no 3, September 1984;

BRITISH ATTITUDES TOWARDS SIX VARIETIES OF ENGLISH IN THE USA AND BRITAIN. Yuko Hiraga, World Englishes, vol 24, no 3, August 2005; **POLITICAL SKILL: EXPLAINING THE EFFECTS OF NONNATIVE ACCENT ON MANERIAL HIRING AND ENTREPRENEURIAL INVESTMENT.** Laura Huang, Marcia Frideger, & Jone L. Pearce, Journal of Applied Psychology, 12 August 2013

11   **INFLUENCE OF COMMUNICATION PARTNER'S GENDER ON LANGUAGE.** Adrienne B. Hancock & Benjamin A. Rubin, Journal of Language and Social Psychology, 11 May 2014; **FEMALE SUPREME COURT JUSTICES ARE INTERRUPTED MORE BY MALE JUSTICE AND ADVOCATES.** Tonja Jacobi & Dyland Schweers, Harvard Business Review, 11 April 2017; **JUSTICE, INTERRUPTED: THE EFFECT OF GENDER, IDEOLOGY AND SENIORTY AT SUPREME COURT ORAL ARGUMENTS.** Tonja Jacobi & Dylan Schweers, Virginia Law Review, 24 October 2017; **GENDER INEQUALITY IN DELIVERATIVE PARTICIPATION.** Christopher F. Karpowitz, Tali Mendelberg, & Lee Shaker, American Political Science Review, pgs 1-15, August 2012; **HOW TO GET AHEAD AS A WOMAN IN TECH: INTERRUPT MEN.** Kieran Snyder, Slate, 23 July 2014; **HOW THE BEST BOSSES INTERRUP BIAS ON THEIR TEAMS.** Joan C. Williams & Sky Mihaylo, Harvard Business Review, November-December 2019; **THE GENDER GAP IS JUST THE TIP OF THE ICEBERG FOR BLACK WOMEN.** Sonya George, Great Place to Work blog, 3 June 2020; **WHITE COLORISM.** Lance Hannon, Social Currents, vol 2, no 1, pgs 13-21, 2015; **MANSPLAINING, EXPLAINED IN ONE SIMPLE CHART.** Kim Goodwin, BBC Worklife, 29 July 2018

12   **WISER: GETTING BEYOND GROUPTHINK TO MAKE GROUPS SMART.** Cass R. Sunstein & Reid Hastie, 2014; **MAKING DUMB GROUPS SMARTER.** Cass R. Sunstein & Reid Hastie, Harvard Business Review, December 2014; **THE SOCIAL ADVANTAGE OF MISCALIBRATED INDIVIDUALS: THE RELATIONSHIP BETWEEN SOCIAL CLASS AND OVERCONFIDENCE AND ITS IMPLICATIONS FOR CLASS-BASED INEQUALITY.** Peter Belmi, Margaret Ann Neale, David Rieff, & Rosemary Ulfe, Journal of Personality & Social Psychology, vol. 118, no 2, pgs 254-282, February 2020; **THE HIDDEN SOCIAL ADVANTAGE.** Corey Binns, Insights by Stanford Business, 26 May 2020

13   **THE DIGITAL SKILLS GAP IS WIDENING FAST. HERE'S HOW TO BRIDGE IT.** Miguel Milano, World Economic Forum Agenda, 12 March 2019; **WHAT IS THE FOURTH INDUSTRIAL REVOLUTION?** Devon McGinnis, Salesforce blog, 20 December 2018; **THE FUTURE OF JOBS REPORT** 2018. World Economic Forum, 2018; **THE GLOBAL COMPETITIVENESS REPORT** 2019. World Economic Forum, 2019; 2019 **STATE OF THE WORKPLACE. SHRM, 2019; CREATING A CULTURE WHERE EMPLOYES SPEAK UP.** Silvia Ann Hewlett, Harvard Business Review, 8 January 2016; **HIDDEN PROFILES: A BRIEF HISTORY.** G. Stasser & W Titus, Psychological Inquiry, vol 14, no 3/4, pgs 304-313, 2003; **WHAT MAKES GREAT BOARDS GREAT.** J. A. Sonnefeld, Harvard Business Review, September 2002; **WHY MANAGERS IGNORE EMPLOYEES' IDEAS.** Elad N. Sherf, Subra Tangirala, & Vijava Venkataramani, Harvard Business Review, 8 April 2019; **AN EXPLORATORY STUDY OF EMPLOYEE SILIENCE: ISSUES THAT EMPLOYEES DON'T COMMUNICATE UPWARD AND WHY.** Frances J. Milliken, Elizabeth W. Morrison, & Patricia F. Hewlin, Journal of Management Studies, 4 August 2003; **CRITICAL UPWARD FEEDBACK IN ORGANISATIONS: PROCESSES, PROBLEMS AND IMPLICATION FOR COMMUNICATION MANAGEMENT.** Dennis Tourish & Paul Robson, Journal of Communication Management, vol 8, no 2, 31 December 2003; **CAN YOUR EMPLOYEES REALLY SPEAK FREELY?** James R. Detert & Ethan Burris, Harvard Business Review, January-February 2016

14   **LEADING A BRAINSTORMING SESSION WITH A CROSS-CULTURAL TEAM.** David Livermore, Harvard Business Review, 27 May 2016; **BIASED EVALUATION OF INFORMATION DURING DISCUSSIONS.** Andreas Mojzisch, Lillia Grouneva, Stefan Schulz-Hardt, European Journal of Social Psychology, vol 40, no 6, 15 September 2010; **BETTER BRAINSTORMING.** Hal Gregersen, Harvard Business Review, March-April 2018; **PSYCHOLOGICAL SAFETY AND LEARNING BEHAVIOUR IN WORK TEAMS.** Amy Edmondson, Administrative Science Quarterly, vol 44, no 2, pgs 350-383; **PRODUCTIVITY LOSS IN BRAINSTORMING GROUPS.** Brian Mullen, Craig Johnson, & Eduardo Salas, Journal of Basic and Applied Social Psychology, vol 12, 1991

15   **WEARING THE CLOAK: ANTECEDENTS AND CONSEQUENCES OF CREATING FACADES OF CONFORMITY.** Patricia Faison Hewlin, Journal of Applied Psychology, vol 94, no 3, pgs 727-741, 2009; **RACE, WORK, AND LEADERSHIP: NEW PERSPECTIVES ON THE BLACK EXPERIENCE**. Edited by Laura Morgan Roberts, Anthony J. Mayo, & David A. Thomas, 13 August 2019; **"DEAR WHITE BOSS..."**. Keith A. Caver & Ancella B. Livers, Harvard Business Review, November 2002; **HOW ORGANIZATIONS ARE FAILING BLACK WORKERS—AND HOW TO DO BETTER.** Adia Harvey Winfield, Harvard Business Review, 16 January 2019; **DIVERSITY AND AUTHENTICITY.** Katherine W. Phillips, Tracy L. Dumas & Nancy P. Rothbard, Harvard Business Review, March-April 2018; **THE BENEFITS OF BRINGING YOUR WHOLE IDENTITY TO WORK.** Sandra E. Cha & Laura Morgan Roberts, Harvard Business Review, 19 September 2019

16   **THE NAME-PRONUNCIATION EFFECT: WHY PEOPLE LIKE MR. SMITH MORE THAN MR. COLQUHOUN.** Simon M. Laham, Peter Koval, Adam L. Atler, Journal of Experimental Social Psychology, vol. 48, no 3, pgs 752-756, May 2012; **DRUNK TANK PINK.** Adam Alter, 2013; **WHAT YOUR NAME SAYS ABOUT HOW BELIEVABLE YOU ARE.** Matti Vuorre, Scientific American, 20 April 2014; **PEOPLE WITH EASIER TO PRONOUNCE NAMES PROMOTE TRUTHINESS OF CLAIMS.** Eryn J. Newman, Mevagh Sanson, Emily K. Miller, Adele Quigley-McBride, Jeffrey L. Foster, Daniel M. Bernstein, & Maryanne Garry, PLOS One, vol 9, no 2, 26 February 2014; **PREDICTING SHORT-TERM STOCK FLUCTUATIONS BY USING PROCESSING FLUENCY.** Adam L. Alter & Daniel M. Oppenheimer, PNAS, vol 103, no 24, pgs 9369-9372, 13 June 2006; **IF ITS DIFFICULT TO PRONOUNCE, IT MUST BE RISKY: FLUENCY, FAMILIARITY, AND RISK PERCEPTION.** Hyunjin Song & Norbert Schwarz, Psychological Science, 1 February 2009

17   **WE ALL KNOW WORKPLACE DIVERSITY MAKES SENSE: SO WHY IS CHANGE SO SLOW?** Tinna Nielsen, World Economic Forum, 14 March 2016; **WOMEN IN THE WORKPLACE.** McKinsey, 2019; **WHY DIVERSITY PROGRAMS FAIL.** Frank Dobbin & Alexandra Kalev, Harvard Business Review, July-August 2016

18   **THE SURPRISING POWER OF SIMPLY ASKING COWORKERS HOW THEY'RE DOING.** Karyn Twaronite, Harvard Business Review, 28 February 2019

19   **NEW STUDY: 3 IN 5 U.S. EMPLOYEES HAVE WITNESSED OR EXPERIENCED DISCRIMINATION.** Glassdoor, 22 October 2019; **DIVERSITY & INCLUSION STUDY** 2019. Glassdoor, 29-31 July 2019

20   **HELP YOUR EMPLOYEES BE THEMSELVES AT WORK.** Dorie Clark & Christie Smith, Harvard Business Review, 3 November 2014

21   **THE GENDER GAP IS JUST THE TIP OF THE ICEBERG FOR BLACK WOMEN.** Sonya George, Great Places to Work, 3 June 2020

22 **HIDING TRUE SELF HARMS CAREER AND SENSE OF BELONGING.** Science Daily, 20 June 2017; **PEOPLE LIKE ME DON'T BELONG HERE: IDENTITY CONCEALMENT IS ASSOCIATED WITH NEGATIVE WORKPLACE EXPERIENCES.** Anna-Kaisa Newheiser, Manuela Barreto, & Jasper Tiermersma, Journal of Social Issues, vol 73, no 2, 2017

23 **THE PANDEMIC HAS EXPOSED THE FALLACY OF THE "IDEAL WORKER".** Joan C. Williams, Harvard Business Review, 11 May 2020

24 **EMPLOYEE ENGAGEMENT CONTINUES HISTORIC RISE AMID CORONAVIRUS.** Jim Harter, Gallup Workplace blog, 29 May 2020

25 **A CHANGING WORLD: GLOBAL VIEWS ON DIVERSITY, GENDER EQUALITY, FAMILY LIFE AND THE IMPORTANCE OF RELIGION.** Jacob Poushter & Janell Fetterolf, Pew Research Center, 22 April 2019

26 **GLOBAL GENDER GAP REPORT 2020.** World Economic Forum, 2020

27 **GLOBAL SOCIAL MOBILITY INDEX 2020: WHY ECONOMIES BENEFIT FROM FIXING INEQUALITY REPORT.** World Economic Forum, 19 January 2020

28 **COVID-19 AND THE WORLD OF WORK: ENSURING NO ONE IS LEFT BEHIND IN THE RESPONSE AND RECOVERY.** International Labour Organisation (ILO), June 2020

29 **WORLD ECONOMIC FORUM GLOBAL RISKS REPORT. 2017, 2018, 2019; THE PSYCHOLOGY OF RADICALIZATION AND DERADICALIZATION: HOW SIGNIFICANCE QUEST IMPACTS VIOLENT EXTREMISM.** A.W. Kruglanski, M. Gelfand, J.J. Bélanger, A. Sheveland, M. Hetiarachchi, & R. Gunaratna, Political Psychology, vol 35, pgs 69-93, 2014; **EDELMAN TRUST BAROMETER.** 2019

30 **RESPONDING TO THE ANGER.** Klaus Schwab, World Economic Forum Agenda, 10 June 2020; **THE GREAT RESET.** Kristalina Georgieva, International Monetary Fund, 3 June 2020

31 **RESPONDING TO THE ANGER.** Klaus Schwab, World Economic Forum Agenda, 10 June 2020

32 **WHY INCLUSIVE LEADERS ARE GOOD FOR ORGANIZATIONS, AND HOW TO BECOME ONE.** Juliet Bourke & Andrea Espedido, Harvard Business Review, 29 March 2019

33 **DEVEOPMENT AS FREEDOM.** Amartya Sen, 2001

34 **WHAT'S GOOD FOR COMPANIES IS GOOD FOR NGOS TOO.** S. Tripathi, livemint, 15 June 2015

35 **THE GREAT RESET.** Kristalina Georgieva, International Monetary Fund, 3 June 2020

36 **NUDGE.** Thaler & Sunstein, pg 6, 2008

37 **THE ASCH CONFORMITY EXPERIMENTS.** Kendra Cherry, Very Well Mind, 5 July 2019

38 **THE DIFFERENCE. HOW DIVERSITY CREATES BETTER GROUPS, FIRMS, SCHOOLS AND SOCIETIES.** Scott E. Page, 2007

39 **THE 4 STAGES OF PSYCHOLOGY SAFETY: DEFINING THE PATH TO INCLUSION AND INNOVATION.** Timothy R Clark, 2020

40 **PSYCHOLOGY CONDITIONS OF PERSONAL ENGAGEMENT AND DISENGAGEMENT AT WORK.** William A. Kahn, Academy of Management Journal, vol 33, no. 4, pgs 692-724, 1990

41 **PSYCHOLOGY SAFETY AND LEARNING BEHAVIOR IN WORK TEAMS.** Amu Edmondson, Administrative Science Quarterly, vol 44, no.2, pgs 350-383, 1999

42 **THE HAPPINESS HYPOTHESIS.** Jonathan Haidt, 2006

43 **LONELINESS AND SOCIAL ISONATION AS RISK FACTORS FOR CORONARY HEART DISEASE AND STROKE.** Nicole K. Valtorta, Mona Kanaan, Simon Gilbody, Sara Ronzi, & Barbara Hanratty, BMJ Heart, vol 102, no 13, pgs 1009-1016, 10 June 2016

44 **WANT TO FEEL HAPPIER TODAY? TRY TALKING TO A STRANGER.** Paul Nicolaus, NPR, 26 July 2019

45 **FIVE HIGHLIGHTS FROM CULTURE AMP'S #CULTUREFIRST CONFERENCE.** Chloe Sesta Jacobs, Medium, 25 June 2018

46 **AMERICAN, SAY MY NAME.** Viet Thanh Nguyen, New York Times, 9 March 2019; **THE STORY OF YOUR NAME.** Katherine Schulten, New York Times, 14 March 2019

47 **THE IMPACT OF THE 'OPEN' WORKSPACE ON HUMAN COLLABORATION.** Ethan S. Bernstein & Stephen Turban, Philosophical Transactions of the Royal Society B, 2 July 2018

48 **WHY IT'S TIME TO DITCH OPEN OFFICE PLANS.** Aytekin Tank, Entrepreneur Europe, 7 February 2019

49 **WORKSPACES THAT MOVE PEOPLE.** Waber, Magnolf & Lindsay, Harvard Business Review, October 2014

50 **PEER STATUS AND CLASSROOM SEATING ARRANGEMENTS: A SOCIAL RELATIONS ANALYSIS.** Yvonne H.M. van den Berg & Antonius H.N. Cillessen, Journal of Experimental Child Psychology, 11 October 2014

51 **PEERS IN PROXIMITY.** Yvonne H.M. van den Berg, 2015

52 ijsfontein's website: https://www.ijsfontein.nl/en/projecten/social-shuffle-2

53 ED Awards website: https://europeandesign.org/submissions/the-social-shuffle/

54 **AMERICAN DEMOCRACY IN CRISIS: THE FATE OF PLURALISM IN A DIVIDED NATION.** Robert P. Jones & Maxine Najle, PRRI, 22 February 2019

55 **BULLYING BECOMES LESS WHEN STUDENTS KNOW EACH OTHER.** Margreet Vermeulen, de Volkskrant, 10 April 2015

56 ED Awards website: https://europeandesign.org/submissions/the-social-shuffle/

57 **RACISM AT WORK.** Binna Kandola, 2018; **RACISM WITHOUT RACISTS: COLOR-BLIND RACISM AND THE PERSISTENCE OF RACIAL INEQUALITY IN AMERICA.** E. Bonilla-Silva, 2010

58 **CAUSAL EFFECT OF INTERGROUP CONTACT ON EXCLUSIONARY ATTITUDES.** Ryan D. Enos, PNAS, vol 111, no 10, pgs 3699-3704, 11 March 2014

59 **DOES RIDING THE COMMUTER RAIL CHANGE ATTITUDES ON IMMIGRATION?** Martine Powers, Boston Globe, 25 February 2014

60 **HOW TO OVERCOME STRESS BY SEEING OTHER PEOPLE'S JOY.** Kelly McGonigal, Greater Good Magazine UC Berkeley, 5 July 2017

61 **WHY MOST PERFORMANCE EVALUATIONS ARE BIASED, AND HOW TO FIX THEM.** Lori Mackenzie, JoAnne Wehner, & Shelley Correll, Harvard Business Review, 11 January 2019

62 **THE PARADOX OF MERITOCRACY IN ORGANIZATIONS.** Emilio J. Castilla & Benard Stephen, Administrative Science Quarterly, vol 55, no 4, pgs 543-676, 2010

63 **ASSESSING PERFORMANCE AND POTENTIAL.** Clayman Institute on Gender at Stanford University, 2015; **THE ABRASIVENESS TRAP: HIGH-ACHIEVING MEN AND WOMEN ARE DESCRIBED DIFFERENTLY IN REVIEWS.** Kieran Synder, Fortune, 24 August 2014; **BIAS IN PERFORMANCE MANAGEMENT REVIEW PROCESS.** Leslie Traub, 2013; **COMBATING GENDER BIAS IN MODERN WORKPLACES.** Alison T. Wynn & Shelley J. Correll, Handbook of the Sociology of Gender, pgs 509-521, 6 June 2018

64 **CASE STUDY: AN INSIDE LOOK AT TELSTRA'S FLEXIBLE WORKING PROGRAM.** Human Resources, 19 July 2017; **CASE STUDY: TELSTRA – ALL ROLES FLEX.** Catalyst, 12 April 2017; **TELSTRA EMPOWERS ITS EMPLOYEES TO DO THEIR BEST WORK FORM ANYWHERE WITH MICROSOFT OFFICE 365.** Gregory Koteras, general manager of digital workplace solutions at Telstra, shares what's worked for Telstra from a technology side to enable all roles flex program, published on the Microsoft website, 17 September 2018

65 **FIRST ADS BANNED FOR CONTRAVENING UK GENDER STEREOTYPING RULES.** Mark Sweney, The Guardian, 14 August 2019

66 **GLOBE WOMEN NEWSLETTER.** no CCXXIX, 24 November 2019

67 **INCREASING RACIAL/ETHNIC DIVERSITY IN NURSING TO REDUCE HEATH DISPARITIES AND ACHIEVE HEALTH EQUITY.** Janice M. Phillips & Beverly Malone, Public Health Reports, vol 129, suppl 2, pgs 45-50, January-February 2014

68 **WHAT EXPLAINS THE RISING SHARE OF U.S. MEN IN REGISTERED NURSING?** Elizabeth Munnich & Abigail Wozinak, Washington Center for Equitable Growth, 3 October 2017

69 **OREGON CENTER FOR NURSING** website, 2019

70 **REPORT EXPLORES WAYS OF ENCOURAGING MEN INTO NURSING.** Grant Hill, University of Dundee Medical Press, 10 August 2018

71 **WHY ARE ONLY ONE IN 10 NURSES MEN?** Louise Cowie, BBC, 2 May 2019

72 **INSIGHT INTO DIVERSITY.** Alexandra Vollman, Nursing Professionals Roundtable, pgs 22-26, January-February 2016

73 **EMPATHY FOR SOCIAL EXCLUSION INVOLVES THE SENSORY-DISCRIMINATIVE COMPONENT OF PAIN: A WITHIN-SUBJECT FMRI STUDY.** G. Novembre, M. Zanon, & G. Silani, SCAN vol 10, pgs 153-164, 2015]

74 **HIDDEN PROFILES: A BRIEF HISTORY.** G. Stasser, & W. Titus, Psychological Inquiry, vol 14, no 3/4, pgs 304–313, 2003

75 **WHAT MAKES GREAT BOARDS GREAT.** J.A. Sonnefeld, Harvard Business Review, September 2002

76 **POP FINANCE: INVESTMENT CLUBS AND THE NEW INVESTOR POPULISM.** B. Harrington, Princeton University Press, 2008

77 **AUTOMATICITY OF SOCIAL BEHAVIOR: DIRECT EFFECTS OF TRAIT CONSTRUCT AND STEREOTYPE ACTIVATION ON ACTION.** John A. Bargh, Mark Chen, and Lara Burrows, Journal of Personality and Social Psychology, 71 (1996): 230-44

78 **FIRMS 'UNDERUTILISING' EMPLOYEES EXISTING SKILLS, REPORT SUGGESTS.** Ashleigh Webber, Personnel Today, 25 February 2020

79 **11 WAYS TO OUTSMART YOUR BRAIN AND BE A BETTER LEADER.** Tinna C. Nielsen & Lisa Kepinski, World Economic Forum Agenda, 3 October 2016

80 **THE HEIGHT LEADERSHIP ADVANTAGE IN MEN AND WOMEN: TESTING EVOLUTIONARY PSYCHOLOGY PREDICTIONS ABOUT THE PERCEPTIONS OF TALL LEADERS.** N.M. Blacker et al., Group Processes Intergroup Relations, vol 16, no 1, pgs 17-27, January 2013

81 **THE POWER OF PERSPECTIVE-TAKING.** Gillian Ku & Kathy Brewis, London Business School Review, 1 February 2017

82 The statement and Daniel Kahneman's inspiration came from: **CLINICAL VERSUS STATISTICAL PREDICTION: A THEORETICAL ANALYSIS AND A REVIEW OF THE EVIDENCE.** Paul E. Meehl, 1954

83 **THINKING, FAST AND SLOW.** Daniel Kahneman, pgs 229-233, 2011

84 **SHE JUST DOESN'T LOOK LIKE A PHILOSOPHER …? AFFECTIVE INFLUENCES ON THE HALO EFFECT IN IMPRESSION FORMATION.** Joseph P. Forgas, European Journal of Social Psychology, vol 41, pgs 812–817, 2011

85 **COLOUR FOR BEHAVIOURAL SUCCESS.** B. Dresp-Langley & A. Reeves, i-Perception, vol 9, no 2, 2018

86 **AN OPPONENT-PROCESS THEORY OF COLOR VISION.** L. M. Hurvich & D. Jameson, Psychological Review, vol 64, pgs 384–505, 1957

87 **PRINCIPLES OF PERCEPTUAL GROUPING: IMPLICATIONS FOR IMAGE-GUIDED SURGERY.** B. Dresp-Langley. Frontiers in Psychology, vol 6, 2015

88 Casciaro & Lobos, 2005

89 **SEEING IS BELIEVING: THE ANTI-INFERENCE BIAS.** Eyal Zamir, Ilana Ritov, & Doron Teichman, Indiana Law Journal, 21 April 2012; **SEEING IS BELIEVING: EXPOSURE TO COUNTERSTEREOTYPIC WOMEN LEADERS AND ITS EFFECT ON THE MALLEABILITY OF AUTOMATIC GENDER STEREOTYPING.** Nilanjana Dasgupta & Shaki Asgari, Journal of Experimental Social Psychology, vol 40, pgs 642-658, 2014

90 Justesen, 2011

91 Gratton et. al., 2007

92 See innoversity.org for more research results

93 **BAKER MCKENZIE FIRST GLOBAL LAW FIRM TO SET 40:40:20 GENDER TARGETS.** Baker McKenzie website, 24 June 2019

94 *Based on several sources including:* Suzanne Justesen, **2011; INNOVATION: WHAT'S DIVERSITY GOT TO DO WITH IT?** Waverly Deutsch, Chicago Booth Review, 14 November 2019

95 **THE FRAMING OF DECISIONS AND THE PSYCHOLOGY OF CHOICE.** Amos Tversky & Daniel Kahneman, Science, vol 211, pgs 453-58, 1981

96 **JUDGEMENT UNDER UNCERTAINTY: HEURISTICS AND BIASES.** Amos Tversky & Daniel Kahneman, Science, vol 185, pgs 1124-31, 1974

97 **BLIND RECRUITMENT TRIAL TO BOOST GENDER EQUALITY MAKING THINGS WORSE, STUDY REVEALS.** Henry Belot, ABC, 30 June 2017; **UNINTENDED EFFECTS OF ANONYMOUS RESUMES.** Luc Behaghel, Bruno Crépon, & Thomas Le Barbanchon, IZA Discussion Papers, no 8517, Institute for the Study of Labor (IZA), Bonn, 2014

98 **HALO EFFECTS.** Joseph P. Forgas & Simon M. Laham, Encyclopedia of Social Psychology, January 2009

99 **BLINDED BY BEAUTY: ATTRACTIVENESS BIAS AND ACCURATE PERCEPTIONS OF ACADEMIC PERFORMANCE.** S.N. Talamas, K.L. Mavor, & D.L. Perrett, PLOS One, vol 11, no 2, 2016

100 **NAME STEREOTYPES AND TEACHERS' EXPECTATIONS** H. Harari, & McDavid, J.W. Journal of Educational Psychology, vol 65, no 2, pgs 222-225, 1973

101 **TOP FLUTIST SETTLES GENDER PAY-GAP SUIT WITH BOSTON SYMPHONY ORCHESTRA.** Anastasia Tsioulcas, NPR, 21 February 2019

102 **THE HAWTHORNE STUDIES.** Historical sources at Harvard University: https://www.library.hbs.edu/hc/hawthorne/rl-selected.html#SDHR

103 **CUES OF BEING WATCHED ENHANCE COOPERATION IN A REAL-WORLD SETTING.** Melissa Bateson, Daniel Nettle, & Gilbert Roberts, Biology Letters, vol 2, pgs 412-4, 2006

104 **SEEING IS BELIEVING: THE ANTI-INFERENCE BIAS.** Eyal Zamir, Ilana Ritov, & Doron Teichman, Indiana Law Journal, 21 April 2012

105 **AWARENESS REDUCES RACIAL BIAS.** Devin G. Pope, Joseph Price, & Justin Wolfers, Management Science, vol 64, no 11, pgs 4988-4995, 2018. NOTE: We do believe that their evidence provides insights that it's not so much 'awareness of bias' but it's seeing the gap between their self-perception as professional referees and their biased behaviour, that helps systems 1 and 2 close the gap and reduce bias in the unconscious, automatic mind (calling the fouls in basketball).

106 **CUES OF BEING WATCHED ENHANCE COOPERATIONS IN A REAL-WORLD SETTING.** Melissa Bateson, Daniel Niettle, & Gilbert Roberts, Biology Letters, vol 2, pgs 412-414, 2016

107 **ACCOUNTABILITY: A SOCIAL CHECK ON THE FUNDAMENTAL ATTRIBUTION ERROR.** Philip E. Tetlock, Social Psychology Quarterly, vol 48, no 3, pgs 227–236, 1985

108 **A FRESH LOOK AT WOMEN NETWORKS GLOBAL SURVEY REPORT.** Veronika Hucke & Lisa Kepinski, January 2016. Report available from the authors.

109 Based on Danish research

110 **WHY WEALTHIER PEOPLE THINK PEOPLE ARE WEALTHIER, AND WHY IT MATTERS.** Rael J. Dawtry, Robbie M. Sutton, & Chris G. Sibley, Psychological Science, 17 July 2015

111 **MINDSPACE: INFLUENCING BEHAVIOUR THROUGH PUBLIC POLICY.** P. Dolan, M. Hallsworth, D. Halpern, D. King, & I. Vlaev, 2010, retrieved 27 September, 2016, from: http://www.instituteforgovernment.org.uk/publications/mindspace

112 **EMPATHY FOR SOCIAL EXCLUSION INVOLVES THE SENSORY-DISCRIMINATIVE COMPONENT OF PAIN: A WITHIN-SUBJECT FMRI STUDY.** G. Novembre, M. Zanon, & G. Silani, SCAN vol 10, pgs 153-164, 2015

113 **JUDGEMENT UNDER UNCERTAINTY: HEURISTICS AND BIASES.** Amos Tversky & Daniel Kahneman, Science, vol 185, no 4157, pgs 1124-1131, 27 September 1974

114 **ARE EXPERIMENTAL ECONOMISTS PRONE TO FRAMING EFFECTS? A NATURAL FIELD EXPERIMENT.** S. Gächter, H. Orzen, E. Renner, & C. Starmer, Journal of Economic Behavior & Organization, vol 70, pgs 443-446, 2009

115 **SINNING SAINTS AND SAINTLY SINNERS: THE PARADOX OF MORAL SELF-REGULATION.** S. Sachdeva, R. Iliev, & D. L. Medin, Psychological Science, 2009

116 **CREATING EQUITY AND BELONGING IN HOW WORK IS DONE.** Veronika Hucke, Founder D&I Strategy & Solutions, and Lisa Kepinski, Founder Inclusion Institute & Co-Founder Inclusion Nudges, August 2019, contact the authors to learn more.

117 **NUDGE.** R. Thaler & C. Sunstein, 2008

118 **INSIDE THE NUDGE UNIT.** David Halpern, pgs 91-92, 2015

119 **EARMARKING AND PARTITIONING: INCREASING SAVING BY LOW-INCOME HOUSEHOLDS.** Dilip Soman & Amar Cheema, Journal of Marketing Research, November 2011

120 **THE CHECKLIST MANIFESTO: HOW TO GET THINGS RIGHT.** Atul Gawande, 2010

121 **RACE, RELIGION, AND POLITICAL AFFILIATION OF AMERICANS' CORE SOCIAL NETWORKS.** Daniel Cox, Juhem Navarro-Rivera, & Robert P. Jones, PRRI, 8 March 2016

122 **AMERICA IS MORE DIVERSE THAN EVER — BUT STILL SEGREGATED.** Aaron Williams & Armand Emamdjomeh, The Washington Post, 10 May 2018

123 **CAN YOU CONNECT WITH ME NOW? HOW THE PRESENCE OF MOBILE COMMUNICATION TECHNOLOGY INFLUENCES FACE-TO-FACE CONVERSATION QUALITY.** Andrew Przybylski & Netta Weinstein, Journal of Social and Personal Relationships, vol 30, pgs 237-246, 2013

124 **CREATING EQUITY AND BELONGING IN HOW WORK IS DONE.** Veronika Hucke, Founder D&I Strategy & Solutions, & Lisa Kepinski, Founder Inclusion Institute & Co-Founder Inclusion Nudges, August 2019, contact the authors to learn more.

125 **THINKING, FAST AND SLOW.** Daniel Kahneman, 2011

126 **DARING GREATLY: HOW THE COURAGE TO BE VULNERABLE TRANSFORMS THE WAY WE LIVE, LOVE, PARENT, AND LEAD.** Brené Brown, 2015

127 **THE DIFFERERENCE. HOW DIVERSITY CREATES BETTER GROUPS, FIRMS, SCHOOLS AND SOCIETIES.** Scott E. Page, 2007

128 https://www.ics.uci.edu/-gmark/chi08-mark.pdf

129 **RETHINKING THE ROLE OF THOUGHT IN SOCIAL INTERACTION.** Ellen J. Langer (1978), New Directions in Attribution Research, vol.2, ed, Harvey, Ickes, & Kidd, 1978.

130 **IMPATIENCE IN TIMING DECISIONS: EFFECTS AND MODERATION.** Moojan Ghafurian & David Reitter, Timing & Time Perception, vol 6, no 2, pgs 183–219, 2018;

A MODEL OF PEDESTRIANS' INTENDED WAITING TIMES FOR STREET CROSSINGS AT SIGNALIZED INTERSECTIONS. Li, Baibing, Transportation Research, Part B: Methodological, 2013

131 **6 WAYS TO SET BOUNDARIES AROUND EMAIL.** Sarah K. Peck, Harvard Business Review, 20 September 2019

132 **MEDICAL DECISION MAKING IN SITUATIONS THAT OFFFER MULTIPE ALTERNATIVES.** D.A. Reidelmeier & E. Shafir, Journal of the American Medical Association, vol 273, pgs 3012-305, 1995

133 **EGO DEPLETION: IS THE ACTIVE SELF A LIMITED RESOURCE?** R.F. Baumeister, E. Bratslavsky, M. Muraven, & D.M. Tice, Journal of Personality and Social Psychology, vol 74, pgs 1252-1265, 1998

134 **DO YOU HAVE A VOTING PLAN?: IMPLEMENTATION INTENTIONS, VOTER TURNOUT, AND ORGANIC PLAN MAKING.** D.W. Nickerson & T. Rogers, Psychology Science, vol 21, no 2, pgs 194–199, 2010

135 **NOBODY'S WATCHING?** K.J. Haley & D.M.T. Fessler, Evolution and Human Behavior, vol 26, pgs 245–256, 2005; **CUES OF BEING WATCHED ENHANCE COOPERATION IN A REAL-WORLD SETTING.** M. Bateson, D. Nettle, & G. Roberts, Biology Letters, vol 2, no 3, pgs 412–414, 2006

136 **STRATEGIES FOR ACHIEVING GOALS IN THE WORKPLACE.** Gail Matthews, Dominican University of California, study presented at the Ninth Annual International Conference of the Psychology Research Unit of Athens Institute for Education and Research (ATINER), May 2015

137 **ACCOUNTING FOR THE EFFECTS OF ACCOUNTABILITY.** J.S. Lerner & P.E. Tetlock, Psychology Bulletin, vol 125, no 2, pgs 255–275, 1999

138 **THE SCIENCE BEHIND SETTING GOALS (AND ACHIEVING THEM).** Forbes Books, 2016

139 **ALAIN ELKANN INTERVIEWS: MINOUCHE SHAFIK.** 1 April 2018

140 **DARING GREATLY: HOW THE COURAGE TO BE VULNERABLE TRANSFORMS THE WAY WE LIVE, LOVE, PARENT, AND LEAD.** Brown, Brené, 2012

141 To review the Creative Commons license, go to: http://creativecommons.org/licenses/by-nc-sa/4.0/

142 While the content is based on the authors' own experience with Inclusion Nudges (the Guidebook, the community, and the website), there was inspiration on this section from Kelly Rae Roberts' website on *'what is and is not okay'* and also from the Global Diversity & Inclusion Benchmark (GDIB) website's permission agreement.

Printed in Great Britain
by Amazon